50 Christmas Lunch Recipes for Home

By: Kelly Johnson

Table of Contents

- Roast Turkey with Herb Stuffing
- Honey Glazed Ham
- Prime Rib Roast
- Cranberry Orange Relish
- Garlic Mashed Potatoes
- Green Bean Casserole
- Roasted Brussels Sprouts with Bacon
- Baked Macaroni and Cheese
- Sweet Potato Casserole
- Cranberry Sauce
- Herb Roasted Pork Tenderloin
- Shrimp Scampi
- Creamed Spinach
- Cornbread Stuffing
- Beef Wellington
- Grilled Salmon with Dill Sauce
- Ratatouille
- Butternut Squash Soup
- Stuffed Mushrooms
- Lemon Garlic Roasted Chicken
- Baked Brie with Cranberry Sauce
- Garlic Parmesan Roasted Potatoes
- Glazed Carrots
- Beef Bourguignon
- Scalloped Potatoes
- Spinach and Artichoke Dip
- Maple Roasted Vegetables
- Caprese Salad
- Herb Crusted Rack of Lamb
- Mushroom Risotto
- Crab Cakes
- Quinoa Salad with Roasted Vegetables
- Roasted Beet Salad with Goat Cheese
- Chicken Piccata
- Pecan Crusted Salmon
- Eggplant Parmesan

- Wild Rice Pilaf
- Antipasto Platter
- Pear and Gorgonzola Salad
- Vegetarian Stuffed Peppers
- Cauliflower Gratin
- Apple Cranberry Walnut Salad
- Beef Stroganoff
- Smoked Gouda Macaroni and Cheese
- Chicken Marsala
- Baked Stuffed Lobster Tails
- Roasted Asparagus with Lemon
- Pistachio Crusted Rack of Lamb
- Tiramisu
- Pecan Pie

Roast Turkey with Herb Stuffing

Ingredients:

For the turkey:

- 1 whole turkey (12-14 pounds)
- Salt and pepper
- 1/2 cup unsalted butter, melted
- 1 tablespoon chopped fresh rosemary
- 1 tablespoon chopped fresh thyme
- 1 tablespoon chopped fresh sage
- 2 cloves garlic, minced
- 1 lemon, halved
- 1 onion, quartered

For the stuffing:

- 1 loaf of bread (about 1 lb), preferably stale, cut into cubes
- 1/2 cup unsalted butter
- 2 onions, finely chopped
- 3-4 celery stalks, finely chopped
- 2-3 cloves garlic, minced
- 2 tablespoons chopped fresh parsley
- 1 tablespoon chopped fresh sage
- 1 tablespoon chopped fresh thyme
- Salt and pepper to taste
- 2-3 cups chicken or turkey broth

Instructions:

1. **Prepare the stuffing:**
    - Preheat oven to 350°F (175°C).
    - Spread bread cubes on a baking sheet and bake until dry and lightly toasted, about 10-15 minutes. Set aside.
    - In a large skillet, melt butter over medium heat. Add onions, celery, and garlic. Cook until onions are translucent and celery is tender, about 5-7 minutes.
    - Stir in parsley, sage, thyme, salt, and pepper. Cook for another 2-3 minutes.
    - Transfer mixture to a large bowl. Add toasted bread cubes and toss to combine. Gradually add chicken or turkey broth until the stuffing is moistened but not soggy.
2. **Prepare the turkey:**
    - Preheat oven to 325°F (165°C). Remove giblets and neck from turkey cavity. Pat dry with paper towels.
    - Season the cavity of the turkey generously with salt and pepper.

- In a small bowl, combine melted butter, rosemary, thyme, sage, and minced garlic.
- Rub the outside of the turkey with the herb butter mixture, making sure to coat evenly.
- Place lemon halves and quartered onion inside the turkey cavity.
- Fill the neck cavity loosely with prepared stuffing. Secure the skin over the stuffing with skewers or kitchen twine.
- Place the turkey breast side up on a rack in a roasting pan. Tent loosely with foil.

3. **Roast the turkey:**
    - Roast in the preheated oven for about 13-15 minutes per pound, or until the internal temperature reaches 165°F (75°C) in the thickest part of the thigh without touching bone.
    - Baste the turkey with pan drippings or additional melted butter every 30 minutes.
    - Remove foil during the last 30 minutes of cooking to allow the skin to brown.

4. **Rest and serve:**
    - Once cooked, transfer the turkey to a cutting board and let it rest for at least 20-30 minutes before carving.
    - Serve with the remaining stuffing and your favorite sides.

Enjoy your delicious roast turkey with herb stuffing for a festive holiday meal!

Honey Glazed Ham

Ingredients:

- 1 bone-in fully cooked ham (7-9 pounds)
- 1 cup honey
- 1/2 cup brown sugar
- 1/4 cup Dijon mustard
- 1/4 cup apple cider vinegar
- 1 tablespoon Worcestershire sauce
- 1/2 teaspoon ground cloves
- 1/2 teaspoon ground cinnamon
- 1/4 teaspoon ground nutmeg

Instructions:

1. **Prepare the glaze:**
   - In a saucepan, combine honey, brown sugar, Dijon mustard, apple cider vinegar, Worcestershire sauce, ground cloves, ground cinnamon, and ground nutmeg.
   - Heat over medium heat, stirring constantly, until the mixture is smooth and the sugar has dissolved. Remove from heat and set aside.
2. **Prepare the ham:**
   - Preheat your oven to 325°F (165°C).
   - Place the ham in a large roasting pan, cut side down.
   - Score the surface of the ham in a diamond pattern with a sharp knife, making cuts about 1/4-inch deep. This helps the glaze penetrate the meat.
3. **Glaze and bake the ham:**
   - Brush or spoon about 1/3 of the glaze mixture over the ham, making sure to get into the scored cuts.
   - Cover the ham loosely with aluminum foil to prevent excessive browning.
   - Bake in the preheated oven for about 1.5 to 2 hours, or until the internal temperature reaches 140°F (60°C) when tested with a meat thermometer, basting with the remaining glaze every 30 minutes.
4. **Rest and serve:**
   - Once cooked, remove the ham from the oven and transfer to a cutting board. Tent loosely with foil and let it rest for about 15 minutes before slicing.
   - Serve slices of honey glazed ham warm, with any remaining glaze drizzled over the top.

Enjoy this delicious honey glazed ham as the centerpiece of your Christmas meal!

Prime Rib Roast

Ingredients:

- 1 standing rib roast (prime rib), about 4-5 pounds, bone-in (you can adjust size based on your needs)
- Salt and freshly ground black pepper
- 4 cloves garlic, minced
- 2 tablespoons olive oil
- 2 tablespoons fresh rosemary, chopped (or 2 teaspoons dried rosemary)
- 2 tablespoons fresh thyme, chopped (or 2 teaspoons dried thyme)

Instructions:

1. **Preparation:**
    - Remove the prime rib roast from the refrigerator about 1-2 hours before cooking to bring it to room temperature. This allows for more even cooking.
    - Preheat your oven to 450°F (230°C).
2. **Seasoning:**
    - Pat the roast dry with paper towels.
    - Rub the entire surface of the roast with olive oil.
    - Season generously with salt and pepper, ensuring an even coating all around.
    - Press minced garlic, chopped rosemary, and chopped thyme onto the surface of the roast, creating a herb crust.
3. **Roasting:**
    - Place the roast, bone side down, on a rack in a roasting pan.
    - Insert a meat thermometer into the thickest part of the roast, making sure it's not touching bone.
    - Roast at 450°F (230°C) for 15 minutes to sear the outside and lock in juices.
    - After 15 minutes, reduce the oven temperature to 325°F (165°C).
4. **Cooking time:**
    - Continue roasting for about 15-20 minutes per pound for medium-rare doneness, or until the internal temperature reaches 120-125°F (49-52°C) for medium-rare or 130-135°F (54-57°C) for medium. Adjust cooking time based on your preferred level of doneness.
    - Baste the roast occasionally with the juices that accumulate in the pan.
5. **Resting:**
    - Once the roast reaches your desired doneness, remove it from the oven and tent loosely with foil.
    - Let the roast rest for at least 15-20 minutes. This allows the juices to redistribute throughout the meat, making it more tender and flavorful.
6. **Slicing and serving:**
    - Carve the prime rib roast into thick slices, following the bone line.
    - Serve warm with your favorite sides like roasted potatoes, Yorkshire pudding, or seasonal vegetables.

Enjoy your beautifully cooked Prime Rib Roast as the centerpiece of your Christmas feast!

Cranberry Orange Relish

Ingredients:

- 12 ounces fresh cranberries, rinsed and picked over
- 1 large orange, zest finely grated and juice squeezed
- 1/2 cup granulated sugar (adjust to taste)
- 1/4 cup water
- Optional: 1/4 cup chopped pecans or walnuts

Instructions:

1. **Prepare the cranberries:**
   - Rinse the fresh cranberries under cold water and remove any stems or debris.
2. **Combine ingredients:**
   - In a medium saucepan, combine the cranberries, finely grated zest of the orange, orange juice, sugar, and water.
   - Optional: Add chopped nuts if desired for texture and flavor.
3. **Cook the relish:**
   - Bring the mixture to a boil over medium-high heat, stirring occasionally.
   - Reduce the heat to medium-low and let it simmer for about 10-15 minutes, or until the cranberries burst and the mixture thickens.
   - Stir occasionally to prevent sticking and burning.
4. **Adjust sweetness:**
   - Taste and adjust sweetness as needed by adding more sugar if desired. Keep in mind that the relish will continue to thicken as it cools.
5. **Cool and serve:**
   - Remove from heat and let the relish cool to room temperature.
   - Transfer to a serving bowl and refrigerate until ready to serve.
6. **Serve:**
   - Serve the Cranberry Orange Relish chilled or at room temperature alongside roasted meats like turkey or ham, or as a festive spread for sandwiches or appetizers.

This Cranberry Orange Relish adds a burst of flavor and vibrant color to your Christmas table, complementing savory dishes with its sweet-tart taste.

Garlic Mashed Potatoes

Ingredients:

- 2 pounds Yukon Gold potatoes, peeled and cut into chunks
- 4 cloves garlic, peeled and smashed
- Salt, to taste
- 1/2 cup unsalted butter, cut into pieces
- 1/2 cup milk (or more as needed)
- 1/4 cup sour cream (optional, for extra creaminess)
- Freshly ground black pepper, to taste
- Chopped fresh chives or parsley, for garnish (optional)

Instructions:

1. **Boil the potatoes:**
    - Place the potato chunks and smashed garlic cloves in a large pot and cover with cold water. Add a generous pinch of salt.
    - Bring to a boil over high heat, then reduce heat to medium-low and simmer until the potatoes are fork-tender, about 15-20 minutes.
2. **Drain and mash:**
    - Drain the potatoes and garlic well in a colander.
    - Return the potatoes and garlic to the pot or a large mixing bowl.
3. **Mash the potatoes:**
    - Use a potato masher or a hand mixer to mash the potatoes and garlic until smooth and lump-free.
4. **Add butter and milk:**
    - While the potatoes are still warm, add the butter pieces to the pot/bowl and stir until melted and incorporated.
    - Gradually add the milk, starting with 1/2 cup, and mix until the potatoes reach your desired creamy consistency. Add more milk if needed.
    - Optional: Stir in sour cream for extra creaminess.
5. **Season:**
    - Season the mashed potatoes with salt and freshly ground black pepper to taste. Adjust seasoning as needed.
6. **Serve:**
    - Transfer the garlic mashed potatoes to a serving bowl.
    - Garnish with chopped fresh chives or parsley if desired.
    - Serve hot as a delicious side dish for your Christmas dinner.

These Garlic Mashed Potatoes are creamy, flavorful, and perfect alongside roasted meats or other festive dishes. Enjoy!

Green Bean Casserole

Ingredients:

- 1 1/2 pounds green beans, trimmed and cut into bite-sized pieces
- 1 can (10.5 ounces) cream of mushroom soup
- 1/2 cup milk
- 1 teaspoon soy sauce
- 1/4 teaspoon black pepper
- 1/4 teaspoon garlic powder
- 1/2 cup crispy fried onions (plus more for topping)
- Optional: 1/2 cup shredded cheddar cheese

Instructions:

1. **Preheat oven:** Preheat your oven to 350°F (175°C). Grease a 2-quart baking dish or casserole dish.
2. **Cook green beans:** Bring a large pot of water to a boil. Add the green beans and cook for about 5 minutes, until just tender-crisp. Drain and rinse with cold water to stop cooking. Set aside.
3. **Prepare the sauce:** In a mixing bowl, whisk together the cream of mushroom soup, milk, soy sauce, black pepper, and garlic powder until well combined.
4. **Combine and bake:**
    - Add the cooked green beans and crispy fried onions to the sauce mixture. Stir gently to coat the green beans evenly.
    - If using, stir in half of the shredded cheddar cheese.
    - Transfer the mixture to the greased baking dish. Spread it out evenly.
5. **Bake:** Cover the dish with foil and bake in the preheated oven for 25-30 minutes, or until bubbly and heated through.
6. **Add toppings and serve:**
    - Remove the foil and sprinkle additional crispy fried onions and remaining shredded cheese (if using) over the top.
    - Return to the oven and bake, uncovered, for an additional 5 minutes or until the onions are golden brown and the cheese is melted.
    - Remove from the oven and let it cool slightly before serving.
7. **Serve:** Serve the Green Bean Casserole warm as a delicious side dish for your Christmas dinner.

This Green Bean Casserole recipe is a comforting and crowd-pleasing addition to any holiday meal, with its creamy sauce and crispy onion topping adding a perfect texture contrast to the tender green beans.

Roasted Brussels Sprouts with Bacon

Ingredients:

- 1.5 pounds Brussels sprouts, trimmed and halved
- 4-6 slices bacon, chopped
- 2 tablespoons olive oil
- Salt and pepper, to taste
- 1/2 teaspoon garlic powder (optional)
- 1/4 cup grated Parmesan cheese (optional)

Instructions:

1. **Preheat oven:** Preheat your oven to 400°F (200°C).
2. **Prepare Brussels sprouts:** Trim the ends of the Brussels sprouts and cut them in half lengthwise. Place them in a large bowl.
3. **Cook bacon:** In a skillet over medium heat, cook the chopped bacon until crispy. Use a slotted spoon to transfer the crispy bacon to a plate lined with paper towels to drain excess fat.
4. **Coat Brussels sprouts:** Drizzle the olive oil over the Brussels sprouts in the bowl. Season with salt, pepper, and garlic powder (if using). Toss until the Brussels sprouts are evenly coated.
5. **Roast Brussels sprouts:** Spread the Brussels sprouts in a single layer on a baking sheet lined with parchment paper or aluminum foil. Make sure they are cut side down as much as possible for caramelization.
6. **Add bacon:** Sprinkle the crispy bacon evenly over the Brussels sprouts.
7. **Roast:** Roast in the preheated oven for 20-25 minutes, or until the Brussels sprouts are tender and caramelized, and the edges are crispy. Stir halfway through roasting for even cooking.
8. **Optional: Add Parmesan cheese:** If desired, sprinkle grated Parmesan cheese over the roasted Brussels sprouts and bacon during the last 5 minutes of baking. This adds extra flavor and richness.
9. **Serve:** Transfer the roasted Brussels sprouts and bacon to a serving dish. Serve hot as a delicious side dish for your Christmas dinner.

This Roasted Brussels Sprouts with Bacon recipe is sure to be a hit at your holiday table, with its crispy bacon adding a smoky flavor that complements the caramelized Brussels sprouts perfectly. Enjoy!

Baked Macaroni and Cheese

Ingredients:

- 12 ounces elbow macaroni (or any pasta shape you prefer)
- 1/4 cup unsalted butter
- 1/4 cup all-purpose flour
- 3 cups whole milk
- 2 cups shredded sharp cheddar cheese
- 1 cup shredded mozzarella cheese
- 1/2 cup grated Parmesan cheese
- Salt and pepper, to taste
- 1/2 teaspoon garlic powder (optional)
- 1/4 teaspoon ground mustard (optional)
- 1/4 teaspoon paprika (optional)
- 1/2 cup breadcrumbs (optional, for topping)

Instructions:

1. **Preheat oven:** Preheat your oven to 350°F (175°C). Grease a 9x13-inch baking dish or a similarly sized casserole dish.
2. **Cook pasta:** Cook the elbow macaroni according to package instructions in a large pot of salted boiling water until al dente. Drain and set aside.
3. **Make cheese sauce:**
    - In the same pot or a separate saucepan, melt the butter over medium heat.
    - Whisk in the flour and cook for 1-2 minutes, stirring constantly, until the mixture turns golden and begins to bubble.
    - Gradually whisk in the milk, stirring constantly to avoid lumps. Cook until the mixture thickens and bubbles, about 5-7 minutes.
    - Remove from heat and stir in the shredded cheddar cheese, mozzarella cheese, and Parmesan cheese until melted and smooth. Season with salt, pepper, garlic powder, ground mustard, and paprika (if using).
4. **Combine pasta and cheese sauce:**
    - Add the cooked macaroni to the cheese sauce and stir until well coated.
5. **Bake:**
    - Pour the macaroni and cheese mixture into the prepared baking dish, spreading it out evenly.
    - Optional: Sprinkle breadcrumbs evenly over the top for a crunchy topping.
6. **Bake:** Bake in the preheated oven for 25-30 minutes, or until the top is golden brown and bubbly.
7. **Serve:** Remove from the oven and let it cool for a few minutes before serving. Serve warm as a delicious side dish for your Christmas dinner.

This Baked Macaroni and Cheese recipe is creamy, cheesy, and irresistible—a perfect complement to your holiday meal. Enjoy!

Sweet Potato Casserole

Ingredients:

For the sweet potatoes:

- 3-4 medium sweet potatoes (about 2 pounds), peeled and cut into chunks
- 1/2 cup milk (whole milk or evaporated milk)
- 1/4 cup unsalted butter, melted
- 1/4 cup brown sugar
- 1 teaspoon vanilla extract
- 1/2 teaspoon ground cinnamon
- 1/4 teaspoon ground nutmeg
- 1/4 teaspoon salt
- 2 large eggs, lightly beaten

For the topping:

- 1/2 cup brown sugar
- 1/3 cup all-purpose flour
- 1/3 cup chopped pecans or walnuts
- 1/4 cup unsalted butter, melted
- Optional: Mini marshmallows for topping (if desired)

Instructions:

1. **Preheat oven:** Preheat your oven to 350°F (175°C). Grease a 9x13-inch baking dish or a similarly sized casserole dish.
2. **Cook sweet potatoes:**
    - Place the sweet potato chunks in a large pot and cover with water. Bring to a boil over medium-high heat.
    - Reduce heat to medium and simmer until the sweet potatoes are tender, about 15-20 minutes. Drain well.
3. **Mash sweet potatoes:**
    - Transfer the cooked sweet potatoes to a large mixing bowl. Mash with a potato masher until smooth.
4. **Prepare the sweet potato mixture:**
    - To the mashed sweet potatoes, add milk, melted butter, brown sugar, vanilla extract, ground cinnamon, ground nutmeg, and salt. Stir until well combined.
    - Gradually add the beaten eggs, stirring continuously, until incorporated into the sweet potato mixture.
5. **Assemble the casserole:**
    - Spread the sweet potato mixture evenly into the prepared baking dish.
6. **Make the topping:**

- In a small bowl, combine brown sugar, flour, chopped pecans or walnuts, and melted butter. Mix until crumbly.
- Sprinkle the topping evenly over the sweet potato mixture.
7. **Optional: Add marshmallows (if desired):**
    - If you prefer a marshmallow topping, sprinkle mini marshmallows over the sweet potato mixture and topping.
8. **Bake:**
    - Bake in the preheated oven for 30-35 minutes, or until the top is golden brown and the casserole is heated through.
    - If using marshmallows, broil for the last 1-2 minutes until marshmallows are golden brown and bubbly, watching closely to prevent burning.
9. **Serve:**
    - Remove from the oven and let it cool slightly before serving.
    - Serve warm as a delicious side dish for your Christmas dinner.

This Sweet Potato Casserole is rich, creamy, and perfectly sweetened—a wonderful addition to your holiday table that everyone will enjoy.

Cranberry Sauce

Ingredients:

- 12 ounces fresh cranberries
- 1 cup granulated sugar
- 1/2 cup orange juice (freshly squeezed is best)
- Zest of 1 orange (optional)
- 1 cinnamon stick (optional)
- 1/4 teaspoon ground cinnamon (optional)

Instructions:

1. **Prepare cranberries:**
    - Rinse the fresh cranberries under cold water and discard any soft or bruised ones.
2. **Cook cranberries:**
    - In a medium saucepan, combine the cranberries, granulated sugar, orange juice, orange zest (if using), and cinnamon stick (if using).
    - Bring the mixture to a boil over medium-high heat.
3. **Simmer:**
    - Reduce the heat to medium-low and simmer, stirring occasionally, until the cranberries burst and the sauce thickens, about 10-15 minutes.
4. **Optional: Add ground cinnamon:**
    - Stir in the ground cinnamon, if using, during the last few minutes of cooking.
5. **Cool and serve:**
    - Remove the saucepan from heat and let the cranberry sauce cool to room temperature.
    - Remove the cinnamon stick, if used, before serving.
6. **Chill (optional):**
    - For a thicker consistency, refrigerate the cranberry sauce for a few hours or overnight before serving.
7. **Serve:**
    - Transfer the cranberry sauce to a serving bowl.
    - Serve chilled or at room temperature as a delicious side dish or condiment for your Christmas dinner.

This homemade Cranberry Sauce is tangy, sweet, and bursting with fresh cranberry flavor—a perfect complement to roasted meats like turkey or ham. Adjust the sweetness to your taste and enjoy the vibrant addition to your holiday feast!

Herb Roasted Pork Tenderloin

Ingredients:

- 2 pork tenderloins (about 1 pound each)
- 2 tablespoons olive oil
- 4 cloves garlic, minced
- 2 teaspoons chopped fresh rosemary
- 2 teaspoons chopped fresh thyme
- 1 teaspoon chopped fresh sage
- 1 teaspoon salt
- 1/2 teaspoon black pepper
- 1/2 teaspoon paprika
- 1/4 teaspoon red pepper flakes (optional, for a bit of heat)
- 1 tablespoon Dijon mustard

Instructions:

1. **Preheat oven:** Preheat your oven to 400°F (200°C).
2. **Prepare the pork tenderloins:**
   - Pat the pork tenderloins dry with paper towels. This helps the seasoning adhere better.
   - In a small bowl, mix together the olive oil, minced garlic, chopped rosemary, thyme, sage, salt, black pepper, paprika, and red pepper flakes (if using).
3. **Season the pork:**
   - Rub the herb and spice mixture all over the pork tenderloins, making sure to coat them evenly.
   - Place the pork tenderloins in a roasting pan or on a baking sheet lined with parchment paper.
4. **Roast the pork:**
   - Roast in the preheated oven for 20-25 minutes, or until the internal temperature reaches 145°F (63°C) using a meat thermometer inserted into the thickest part of the tenderloin.
   - Optionally, you can brush the pork tenderloins with Dijon mustard during the last 5-10 minutes of cooking for added flavor and a beautiful glaze.
5. **Rest and serve:**
   - Remove the pork tenderloins from the oven and tent loosely with foil. Let them rest for 5-10 minutes. This allows the juices to redistribute and the meat to finish cooking.
6. **Slice and serve:**
   - Slice the herb roasted pork tenderloin into thick slices.
   - Serve warm with your favorite sides like roasted vegetables, mashed potatoes, or a fresh salad.

This Herb Roasted Pork Tenderloin is tender, juicy, and infused with the flavors of garlic and fresh herbs—a perfect centerpiece for your Christmas dinner that's sure to impress your guests. Enjoy!

Shrimp Scampi

Ingredients:

- 1 pound large shrimp, peeled and deveined
- Salt and pepper, to taste
- 4 tablespoons unsalted butter
- 4 tablespoons olive oil
- 4 cloves garlic, minced
- 1/4 teaspoon red pepper flakes (adjust to taste)
- 1/4 cup white wine (such as Pinot Grigio or Sauvignon Blanc)
- Juice of 1 lemon
- Zest of 1 lemon
- 1/4 cup chopped fresh parsley
- Cooked pasta or crusty bread, for serving

Instructions:

1. **Prepare the shrimp:**
   - Pat the shrimp dry with paper towels and season with salt and pepper to taste.
2. **Cook the shrimp:**
   - In a large skillet, heat 2 tablespoons of butter and 2 tablespoons of olive oil over medium-high heat.
   - Add the shrimp to the skillet in a single layer (you may need to do this in batches depending on the size of your skillet). Cook the shrimp for about 2 minutes per side, until they are pink and opaque. Remove the shrimp from the skillet and set aside.
3. **Make the sauce:**
   - In the same skillet, add the remaining 2 tablespoons of butter and 2 tablespoons of olive oil.
   - Add the minced garlic and red pepper flakes. Cook for 1-2 minutes, stirring constantly, until the garlic is fragrant and lightly golden.
4. **Deglaze the skillet:**
   - Pour in the white wine and scrape any browned bits from the bottom of the skillet with a wooden spoon. Let the wine simmer for 2-3 minutes until slightly reduced.
5. **Finish the dish:**
   - Stir in the lemon juice and lemon zest.
   - Return the cooked shrimp to the skillet and toss to coat with the sauce.
   - Cook for an additional 1-2 minutes, until the shrimp are heated through and coated with the sauce.
   - Remove from heat and stir in the chopped parsley.
6. **Serve:**
   - Serve the shrimp scampi immediately over cooked pasta or with crusty bread to soak up the delicious sauce.
   - Garnish with additional chopped parsley and lemon wedges if desired.

This Shrimp Scampi recipe is flavorful, tangy, and quick to prepare—making it a perfect dish to impress your guests during your Christmas dinner. Enjoy!

Creamed Spinach

Ingredients:

- 2 pounds fresh spinach leaves, washed and trimmed
- 2 tablespoons unsalted butter
- 2 cloves garlic, minced
- 1/4 cup all-purpose flour
- 1 cup heavy cream
- 1/2 cup milk (whole milk or half-and-half)
- 1/4 teaspoon ground nutmeg
- Salt and pepper, to taste
- 1/4 cup grated Parmesan cheese (optional, for extra flavor)

Instructions:

1. **Prepare the spinach:**
    - If the spinach leaves are large, chop them roughly.
    - Blanch the spinach in a pot of boiling water for 1-2 minutes, until wilted. Drain and immediately rinse with cold water to stop the cooking process. Squeeze out excess water from the spinach using paper towels or a clean kitchen towel. Chop finely and set aside.
2. **Make the cream sauce:**
    - In a large skillet or saucepan, melt the butter over medium heat.
    - Add the minced garlic and sauté for 1-2 minutes, until fragrant.
3. **Thicken the sauce:**
    - Stir in the flour and cook for 1-2 minutes, stirring constantly, to form a roux.
4. **Add the cream and milk:**
    - Gradually pour in the heavy cream and milk, stirring constantly to prevent lumps.
    - Cook the mixture for 3-4 minutes, until it begins to thicken.
5. **Season and finish:**
    - Stir in the ground nutmeg, salt, and pepper to taste.
    - Add the chopped spinach to the cream sauce, stirring well to combine.
    - Cook for an additional 2-3 minutes, until the spinach is heated through and the sauce has thickened to your desired consistency.
    - Optional: Stir in grated Parmesan cheese for extra flavor.
6. **Serve:**
    - Transfer the creamed spinach to a serving dish.
    - Serve warm as a delicious and creamy side dish for your Christmas dinner.

This Creamed Spinach recipe is smooth, creamy, and packed with flavor—a perfect addition to your holiday table that will impress your guests. Enjoy!

Cornbread Stuffing

Ingredients:

- 1 batch of cornbread (about 8 cups, crumbled) - you can use store-bought or homemade cornbread
- 1/2 cup unsalted butter
- 1 large onion, diced
- 3-4 celery stalks, diced
- 2-3 cloves garlic, minced
- 1 teaspoon dried sage
- 1 teaspoon dried thyme
- 1/2 teaspoon dried rosemary
- Salt and pepper, to taste
- 2-3 cups low-sodium chicken or vegetable broth
- 2 large eggs, beaten
- 1/2 cup chopped fresh parsley (optional, for garnish)

Instructions:

1. **Prepare the cornbread:**
   - If using homemade cornbread, bake it ahead of time according to your favorite recipe or use store-bought cornbread. Allow it to cool completely, then crumble it into a large mixing bowl.
2. **Preheat oven:** Preheat your oven to 350°F (175°C). Grease a 9x13-inch baking dish or a similarly sized casserole dish.
3. **Saute the vegetables:**
   - In a large skillet, melt the butter over medium heat.
   - Add the diced onion and celery. Cook until softened, about 5-7 minutes.
   - Add the minced garlic, dried sage, dried thyme, and dried rosemary. Cook for an additional 1-2 minutes until fragrant. Season with salt and pepper to taste.
4. **Combine ingredients:**
   - Transfer the sautéed vegetables to the bowl with the crumbled cornbread. Mix well to combine.
5. **Moisten with broth:**
   - Gradually add the chicken or vegetable broth to the cornbread mixture, stirring gently to moisten. The amount of broth you use will depend on how moist you like your stuffing. Start with 2 cups and add more as needed.
6. **Add eggs:**
   - Stir in the beaten eggs until well combined. This helps bind the stuffing together during baking.
7. **Transfer to baking dish:**
   - Transfer the cornbread stuffing mixture to the prepared baking dish, spreading it out evenly.
8. **Bake:**

- Cover the baking dish with foil and bake in the preheated oven for 30-40 minutes, or until the stuffing is heated through and the top is golden brown.
9. **Optional: Garnish and serve:**
    - If desired, garnish the cornbread stuffing with chopped fresh parsley before serving.
10. **Serve warm:**
    - Serve the cornbread stuffing warm as a delicious side dish for your Christmas dinner.

This Cornbread Stuffing recipe is savory, aromatic, and perfect alongside roasted meats and other holiday dishes. Enjoy the comforting flavors and textures that this classic dish brings to your holiday table!

Beef Wellington

Ingredients:

- 1 1/2 to 2 pounds beef tenderloin, trimmed
- Salt and freshly ground black pepper
- 2 tablespoons olive oil
- 2 tablespoons Dijon mustard
- 8-10 slices prosciutto or thinly sliced ham
- 1 package (17.3 ounces) frozen puff pastry, thawed (or homemade puff pastry)
- 1/2 cup pâté or mushroom duxelles (optional)
- 1 egg, beaten (for egg wash)

Instructions:

1. **Preheat oven:** Preheat your oven to 425°F (220°C). Line a baking sheet with parchment paper.
2. **Prepare the beef:**
   - Pat the beef tenderloin dry with paper towels. Season generously with salt and pepper.
3. **Sear the beef:**
   - In a large skillet, heat the olive oil over high heat until hot but not smoking.
   - Sear the beef tenderloin on all sides until nicely browned, about 2-3 minutes per side. Remove from heat and let it cool slightly.
4. **Coat with mustard and prosciutto:**
   - Brush the seared beef tenderloin with Dijon mustard all over.
   - Lay the slices of prosciutto or thinly sliced ham on a sheet of plastic wrap, slightly overlapping, to create a layer large enough to wrap around the beef tenderloin.
5. **Wrap the beef:**
   - Place the beef tenderloin in the center of the prosciutto or ham slices. Using the plastic wrap, roll the prosciutto or ham tightly around the beef tenderloin, pressing to adhere. Discard the plastic wrap.
6. **Roll out the puff pastry:**
   - On a lightly floured surface, roll out the puff pastry to a size large enough to completely wrap the beef tenderloin.
7. **Assemble the Wellington:**
   - If using pâté or mushroom duxelles, spread a thin layer over the prosciutto or ham-wrapped beef tenderloin.
   - Place the wrapped beef tenderloin in the center of the puff pastry. Fold the puff pastry over the beef, sealing the edges by pressing with your fingers. Trim any excess pastry if necessary.
8. **Brush with egg wash:**
   - Transfer the beef Wellington to the prepared baking sheet, seam side down.
   - Brush the entire surface of the puff pastry with beaten egg to create a golden crust when baked.

9. **Bake:**
    - Bake in the preheated oven for 35-40 minutes, or until the puff pastry is golden brown and the beef reaches an internal temperature of 125°F (for medium-rare) to 135°F (for medium) using a meat thermometer.
10. **Rest and serve:**
    - Remove from the oven and let the beef Wellington rest for 10 minutes before slicing.
    - Slice into thick portions and serve warm, garnished with fresh herbs if desired.

Beef Wellington is a decadent and impressive dish that's sure to impress your guests at Christmas dinner. Enjoy the tender beef wrapped in flavorful prosciutto and encased in golden, flaky puff pastry!

Grilled Salmon with Dill Sauce

Ingredients:

- 4 salmon fillets (about 6 ounces each), skin-on or skinless
- Salt and pepper, to taste
- 2 tablespoons olive oil

For the Dill Sauce:

- 1/2 cup sour cream or Greek yogurt
- 2 tablespoons mayonnaise
- 1 tablespoon fresh dill, chopped (or 1 teaspoon dried dill)
- 1 tablespoon fresh lemon juice
- 1 teaspoon Dijon mustard
- Salt and pepper, to taste

Instructions:

1. **Prepare the salmon:**
    - Pat the salmon fillets dry with paper towels. Season both sides with salt and pepper to taste.
2. **Preheat the grill:**
    - Preheat your grill to medium-high heat. Brush the grates lightly with oil to prevent sticking.
3. **Grill the salmon:**
    - Brush the salmon fillets with olive oil on both sides.
    - Place the salmon fillets on the preheated grill, skin-side down if they have skin. Grill for 4-5 minutes per side, or until the salmon is cooked through and easily flakes with a fork. Cooking time will vary depending on the thickness of the fillets.
4. **Make the dill sauce:**
    - While the salmon is grilling, prepare the dill sauce. In a small bowl, whisk together the sour cream or Greek yogurt, mayonnaise, chopped dill, lemon juice, and Dijon mustard until smooth.
    - Season with salt and pepper to taste. Adjust the lemon juice and dill according to your preference.
5. **Serve:**
    - Remove the grilled salmon from the grill and transfer to a serving platter or individual plates.
    - Spoon the dill sauce over the grilled salmon fillets, or serve it on the side as a dipping sauce.
    - Garnish with additional fresh dill, lemon slices, or parsley if desired.
6. **Enjoy:**
    - Serve the Grilled Salmon with Dill Sauce immediately while warm. It pairs well with steamed vegetables, rice, or a fresh salad.

This Grilled Salmon with Dill Sauce recipe is quick to prepare and full of fresh, vibrant flavors—perfect for a special holiday meal like Christmas. Enjoy the tender and flaky salmon with the creamy and tangy dill sauce!

Ratatouille

Ingredients:

- 1 large eggplant, diced
- 2 zucchinis, diced
- 1 yellow bell pepper, diced
- 1 red bell pepper, diced
- 1 onion, diced
- 4 cloves garlic, minced
- 4 tomatoes, diced (or 1 can (14 oz) diced tomatoes)
- 2 tablespoons tomato paste
- 2 tablespoons olive oil
- 1 teaspoon dried thyme
- 1 teaspoon dried oregano
- Salt and pepper, to taste
- Fresh basil or parsley, chopped, for garnish

Instructions:

1. **Prepare the vegetables:**
   - Dice the eggplant, zucchinis, yellow bell pepper, red bell pepper, onion, and tomatoes. Mince the garlic.
2. **Saute the vegetables:**
   - In a large skillet or Dutch oven, heat the olive oil over medium heat.
   - Add the diced onion and sauté for 3-4 minutes until softened and translucent.
   - Add the minced garlic and sauté for another 1-2 minutes until fragrant.
3. **Cook the vegetables:**
   - Add the diced eggplant, zucchinis, yellow bell pepper, and red bell pepper to the skillet.
   - Cook, stirring occasionally, for 8-10 minutes until the vegetables start to soften.
4. **Add tomatoes and seasonings:**
   - Stir in the diced tomatoes (with their juices) and tomato paste.
   - Add dried thyme, dried oregano, salt, and pepper to taste. Stir well to combine.
5. **Simmer:**
   - Reduce the heat to low, cover the skillet, and let the ratatouille simmer for 20-25 minutes, stirring occasionally, until all the vegetables are tender and the flavors have melded together.
6. **Adjust seasoning and serve:**
   - Taste and adjust seasoning if needed with more salt and pepper.
   - Remove from heat and garnish with chopped fresh basil or parsley.
7. **Serve:**
   - Serve the ratatouille warm as a main dish or side dish. It pairs well with crusty bread, rice, or quinoa.

Ratatouille can be made ahead of time and reheats well, allowing you to prepare it in advance for your Christmas dinner. It's a hearty and satisfying dish that celebrates the flavors of fresh vegetables in a rich and aromatic tomato base. Enjoy this traditional French recipe with your loved ones!

Butternut Squash Soup

Ingredients:

- 1 large butternut squash (about 3 pounds), peeled, seeded, and diced
- 2 tablespoons olive oil
- 1 onion, chopped
- 2 carrots, peeled and chopped
- 2 celery stalks, chopped
- 4 cloves garlic, minced
- 4 cups vegetable broth (or chicken broth)
- 1 teaspoon dried thyme
- 1/2 teaspoon ground cinnamon
- 1/4 teaspoon ground nutmeg
- Salt and pepper, to taste
- 1/2 cup heavy cream or coconut milk (for a dairy-free option)
- Optional garnish: Fresh thyme, pepitas (pumpkin seeds), drizzle of cream or coconut milk

Instructions:

1. **Prepare the butternut squash:**
   - Peel the butternut squash using a vegetable peeler. Cut it in half lengthwise, scoop out the seeds with a spoon, and dice the flesh into cubes.
2. **Saute the vegetables:**
   - In a large pot or Dutch oven, heat the olive oil over medium heat.
   - Add the chopped onion, carrots, and celery. Cook for 5-7 minutes, stirring occasionally, until the vegetables begin to soften.
3. **Add garlic and spices:**
   - Add the minced garlic, dried thyme, ground cinnamon, and ground nutmeg to the pot. Cook for 1-2 minutes until fragrant.
4. **Cook the squash:**
   - Add the diced butternut squash to the pot and stir to combine with the other vegetables and spices.
5. **Simmer:**
   - Pour in the vegetable broth (or chicken broth) to cover the vegetables. Bring the mixture to a boil, then reduce the heat to medium-low. Cover and simmer for 20-25 minutes, or until the butternut squash is tender and easily pierced with a fork.
6. **Blend the soup:**
   - Use an immersion blender directly in the pot to blend the soup until smooth and creamy. Alternatively, carefully transfer the soup in batches to a blender and blend until smooth. Be cautious with hot liquids.
7. **Add cream and season:**

- Stir in the heavy cream or coconut milk to add richness to the soup. Season with salt and pepper to taste. Adjust the consistency with more broth or water if desired.
8. **Serve:**
    - Ladle the butternut squash soup into bowls. Garnish with a drizzle of cream or coconut milk, fresh thyme leaves, and pepitas (pumpkin seeds) for added texture and flavor.
9. **Enjoy:**
    - Serve the butternut squash soup warm as a comforting appetizer or main dish for your Christmas dinner.

This Butternut Squash Soup recipe is creamy, flavorful, and showcases the natural sweetness of butternut squash with warm spices. It's a delightful addition to your holiday menu, providing a cozy and satisfying dish for your guests to enjoy.

Stuffed Mushrooms

Ingredients:

- 24 large button mushrooms, stems removed and reserved
- 1 tablespoon olive oil
- 2 cloves garlic, minced
- 1/2 onion, finely chopped
- 1/2 cup breadcrumbs (plain or seasoned)
- 1/4 cup grated Parmesan cheese
- 1/4 cup chopped fresh parsley
- Salt and pepper, to taste
- Optional: 1/4 cup chopped cooked bacon or pancetta
- Optional: 1/4 cup shredded mozzarella or cheddar cheese for topping

Instructions:

1. **Prepare the mushrooms:**
   - Preheat your oven to 375°F (190°C). Line a baking sheet with parchment paper.
   - Remove the stems from the mushrooms and finely chop them. Set the mushroom caps aside.
2. **Prepare the filling:**
   - In a skillet, heat the olive oil over medium heat. Add the chopped mushroom stems and cook for 3-4 minutes until they begin to soften.
   - Add the minced garlic and chopped onion to the skillet. Cook for another 2-3 minutes until the onion is translucent and fragrant.
3. **Make the stuffing mixture:**
   - Remove the skillet from heat and stir in the breadcrumbs, grated Parmesan cheese, chopped parsley, salt, and pepper. If using, add the optional cooked bacon or pancetta. Mix well to combine.
4. **Stuff the mushrooms:**
   - Spoon the filling mixture into each mushroom cap, pressing lightly to pack the filling.
5. **Bake the stuffed mushrooms:**
   - Arrange the stuffed mushrooms on the prepared baking sheet.
   - If desired, sprinkle shredded mozzarella or cheddar cheese on top of each stuffed mushroom.
6. **Bake in the preheated oven:**
   - Bake for 20-25 minutes, or until the mushrooms are tender and the filling is golden brown and crispy on top.
7. **Serve warm:**
   - Remove from the oven and let the stuffed mushrooms cool slightly before serving.
   - Garnish with additional chopped parsley if desired.

These Stuffed Mushrooms are savory, flavorful, and perfect for entertaining. They can be prepared ahead of time and baked just before serving, making them a convenient and tasty addition to your Christmas dinner menu. Enjoy these delicious bites with your guests!

Lemon Garlic Roasted Chicken

Ingredients:

- 1 whole chicken (about 4-5 pounds), giblets removed
- Salt and pepper, to taste
- 2 tablespoons olive oil
- 4 cloves garlic, minced
- Zest of 1 lemon
- Juice of 1 lemon
- 1 tablespoon fresh thyme leaves (or 1 teaspoon dried thyme)
- 1 tablespoon fresh rosemary leaves (or 1 teaspoon dried rosemary)
- 1 tablespoon fresh parsley, chopped (optional, for garnish)

Instructions:

1. **Preheat the oven:** Preheat your oven to 400°F (200°C). Place a rack in the middle of the oven.
2. **Prepare the chicken:**
   - Pat the chicken dry with paper towels inside and out. Season the cavity generously with salt and pepper.
   - Tie the legs together with kitchen twine and tuck the wing tips under the body of the chicken.
3. **Make the lemon garlic marinade:**
   - In a small bowl, combine the olive oil, minced garlic, lemon zest, lemon juice, thyme, and rosemary. Stir well to mix.
4. **Season the chicken:**
   - Place the chicken on a roasting pan or baking dish. Rub the lemon garlic mixture all over the chicken, ensuring it's evenly coated. Season the outside of the chicken generously with salt and pepper.
5. **Roast the chicken:**
   - Roast the chicken in the preheated oven for 1 hour to 1 hour 15 minutes, or until the internal temperature reaches 165°F (75°C) in the thickest part of the thigh, away from the bone.
6. **Baste the chicken:**
   - Every 20-30 minutes during roasting, baste the chicken with the juices that collect in the pan. This helps keep the chicken moist and flavorful.
7. **Rest and serve:**
   - Once cooked, remove the chicken from the oven and let it rest for 10-15 minutes before carving.
   - Garnish with chopped fresh parsley, if desired.
8. **Carve and enjoy:**
   - Carve the lemon garlic roasted chicken into pieces and serve warm with your favorite side dishes like roasted vegetables, potatoes, or a fresh salad.

This Lemon Garlic Roasted Chicken is juicy, flavorful, and aromatic—perfect for a special holiday meal like Christmas. The combination of lemon, garlic, and herbs infuses the chicken with delicious flavors that your family and guests will love.

Baked Brie with Cranberry Sauce

Ingredients:

- 1 wheel of Brie cheese (about 8-10 ounces)
- 1/2 cup cranberry sauce (homemade or store-bought)
- 1/4 cup chopped pecans or walnuts (optional)
- 1 tablespoon honey (optional, for drizzling)
- Crackers, sliced baguette, or apple slices, for serving

Instructions:

1. **Preheat the oven:** Preheat your oven to 350°F (175°C).
2. **Prepare the Brie:**
   - Place the Brie wheel on a baking sheet lined with parchment paper or in a Brie baker.
3. **Top with cranberry sauce:**
   - Spread the cranberry sauce evenly over the top of the Brie wheel.
4. **Optional toppings:**
   - Sprinkle chopped pecans or walnuts over the cranberry sauce.
   - Drizzle honey over the top for added sweetness, if desired.
5. **Bake the Brie:**
   - Bake the Brie in the preheated oven for 10-15 minutes, or until the cheese is soft and gooey, and the cranberry sauce is warm and slightly bubbly.
6. **Serve:**
   - Remove the baked Brie from the oven and let it cool for a few minutes.
   - Serve warm with crackers, sliced baguette, or apple slices for dipping.
7. **Enjoy:**
   - Enjoy the creamy, melted Brie with the sweet and tangy cranberry sauce. It's a perfect appetizer to impress your guests at Christmas or any special occasion.

This Baked Brie with Cranberry Sauce recipe is quick to prepare and offers a delightful combination of flavors and textures. It's sure to be a hit at your holiday gathering!

Garlic Parmesan Roasted Potatoes

Ingredients:

- 2 pounds baby potatoes (red or gold), halved or quartered if large
- 3 tablespoons olive oil
- 4 cloves garlic, minced
- 1 teaspoon dried thyme
- 1/2 teaspoon dried rosemary
- Salt and pepper, to taste
- 1/2 cup grated Parmesan cheese
- Fresh parsley, chopped (optional, for garnish)

Instructions:

1. **Preheat the oven:** Preheat your oven to 400°F (200°C). Line a baking sheet with parchment paper or foil for easy cleanup.
2. **Prepare the potatoes:**
   - Wash and dry the baby potatoes. If they are larger, halve or quarter them so they cook evenly.
3. **Make the seasoning mixture:**
   - In a small bowl, combine the olive oil, minced garlic, dried thyme, dried rosemary, salt, and pepper. Stir well to mix.
4. **Coat the potatoes:**
   - Place the potatoes on the prepared baking sheet. Drizzle the olive oil mixture over the potatoes, tossing to coat them evenly.
5. **Roast the potatoes:**
   - Spread the potatoes out in a single layer on the baking sheet.
   - Roast in the preheated oven for 30-35 minutes, stirring halfway through, until the potatoes are golden and crispy on the outside, and tender on the inside.
6. **Add Parmesan cheese:**
   - Sprinkle the grated Parmesan cheese evenly over the roasted potatoes during the last 5 minutes of baking. This allows the cheese to melt and become golden.
7. **Garnish and serve:**
   - Remove the roasted potatoes from the oven.
   - Garnish with chopped fresh parsley, if desired, for a pop of color and added freshness.
8. **Enjoy:**
   - Serve the Garlic Parmesan Roasted Potatoes warm as a delicious side dish for your Christmas dinner.

These Garlic Parmesan Roasted Potatoes are flavorful, crispy on the outside, and creamy on the inside—perfect for complementing roasted meats or poultry during the holiday season. They are sure to be a crowd-pleaser at your festive gathering!

Glazed Carrots

Ingredients:

- 1 pound carrots, peeled and sliced into rounds or sticks
- 2 tablespoons unsalted butter
- 1/4 cup brown sugar
- 1/4 cup water or vegetable broth
- Salt and pepper, to taste
- Fresh parsley or dill, chopped (optional, for garnish)

Instructions:

1. **Prepare the carrots:**
   - Peel the carrots and slice them into rounds or sticks, depending on your preference.
2. **Cook the carrots:**
   - In a large skillet or saucepan, melt the butter over medium heat.
   - Add the sliced carrots to the skillet and sauté for 2-3 minutes, stirring occasionally, until they start to soften.
3. **Make the glaze:**
   - Sprinkle the brown sugar over the carrots and stir to coat evenly.
   - Pour in the water or vegetable broth. Stir to combine.
4. **Simmer:**
   - Bring the mixture to a simmer. Reduce the heat to medium-low and cover the skillet with a lid.
   - Let the carrots simmer for 10-15 minutes, or until they are tender and the liquid has reduced to a glaze, stirring occasionally.
5. **Season and serve:**
   - Season the glazed carrots with salt and pepper to taste.
   - Garnish with chopped fresh parsley or dill, if desired, for a pop of color and freshness.
6. **Enjoy:**
   - Serve the Glazed Carrots warm as a delicious and vibrant side dish for your Christmas dinner.

These Glazed Carrots are tender, sweet, and beautifully shiny from the brown sugar glaze—a perfect complement to roasted meats or poultry during the holiday season. They add a festive touch to your table and are sure to be enjoyed by your family and guests!

Beef Bourguignon

Ingredients:

- 2 pounds beef chuck roast, cut into 1-inch cubes
- Salt and pepper, to taste
- 3 tablespoons olive oil, divided
- 4 ounces bacon, diced
- 1 onion, chopped
- 2 carrots, peeled and sliced
- 2 cloves garlic, minced
- 2 tablespoons all-purpose flour
- 1 bottle (750 ml) red wine, such as Pinot Noir or Burgundy
- 2 cups beef broth
- 2 tablespoons tomato paste
- 1 teaspoon dried thyme
- 2 bay leaves
- 1 pound pearl onions, peeled
- 1 pound mushrooms, sliced
- Fresh parsley, chopped, for garnish

Instructions:

1. **Preheat the oven:** Preheat your oven to 325°F (160°C).
2. **Prepare the beef:**
   - Pat the beef cubes dry with paper towels. Season generously with salt and pepper.
3. **Brown the beef:**
   - In a large Dutch oven or heavy-bottomed pot, heat 2 tablespoons of olive oil over medium-high heat.
   - Add the beef cubes in batches and brown on all sides. Transfer the browned beef to a plate and set aside.
4. **Cook the bacon and vegetables:**
   - In the same pot, add the diced bacon and cook until crispy. Remove the bacon with a slotted spoon and set aside.
   - Add the chopped onion and sliced carrots to the pot. Cook for 5-7 minutes, stirring occasionally, until the onions are translucent and the carrots start to soften.
   - Add the minced garlic and cook for an additional minute until fragrant.
5. **Make the stew:**
   - Sprinkle the flour over the vegetables in the pot. Stir to coat evenly and cook for 1-2 minutes.
   - Slowly pour in the red wine and beef broth, stirring constantly to deglaze the bottom of the pot.
   - Stir in the tomato paste, dried thyme, and bay leaves.

6. **Add the beef and simmer:**
    - Return the browned beef and any juices to the pot. Bring the mixture to a simmer.
7. **Bake in the oven:**
    - Cover the pot with a lid and transfer it to the preheated oven. Bake for 2 to 2 1/2 hours, or until the beef is tender and the flavors have melded together.
8. **Prepare the mushrooms and pearl onions:**
    - While the stew is baking, heat the remaining 1 tablespoon of olive oil in a skillet over medium heat.
    - Add the pearl onions and cook for 10-12 minutes, or until they are caramelized and tender. Remove from the skillet and set aside.
    - In the same skillet, add the sliced mushrooms and cook for 5-7 minutes, or until they are golden brown and softened. Remove from heat and set aside.
9. **Finish the stew:**
    - Once the stew is done baking, remove it from the oven.
    - Stir in the cooked bacon, caramelized pearl onions, and sautéed mushrooms.
    - Taste and adjust seasoning with salt and pepper if needed.
10. **Serve:**
    - Discard the bay leaves. Serve Beef Bourguignon hot, garnished with chopped fresh parsley.

Beef Bourguignon is traditionally served with mashed potatoes, crusty bread, or over egg noodles to soak up the delicious sauce. It's a comforting and luxurious dish that's sure to impress your guests during the holiday season. Enjoy this classic French stew as the centerpiece of your Christmas dinner!

Scalloped Potatoes

Ingredients:

- 2 pounds Yukon Gold potatoes, peeled and thinly sliced (about 1/8-inch thick)
- 2 tablespoons unsalted butter
- 2 tablespoons all-purpose flour
- 2 cups whole milk
- 1 cup heavy cream
- 2 cloves garlic, minced
- 1 teaspoon dried thyme (or 1 tablespoon fresh thyme leaves)
- 1/2 teaspoon salt, or more to taste
- 1/4 teaspoon black pepper, or more to taste
- 1 1/2 cups shredded Gruyère cheese (or Swiss cheese)
- 1/2 cup grated Parmesan cheese
- Fresh parsley, chopped, for garnish

Instructions:

1. **Preheat the oven:** Preheat your oven to 375°F (190°C). Butter a 9x13-inch baking dish or a similar-sized casserole dish.
2. **Prepare the potatoes:**
   - Peel the potatoes and thinly slice them into rounds, about 1/8-inch thick. You can use a mandoline slicer for even slices, if available.
3. **Make the sauce:**
   - In a medium saucepan, melt the butter over medium heat.
   - Add the minced garlic and cook for 1 minute until fragrant.
   - Stir in the flour and cook for another 1-2 minutes, stirring constantly, to make a roux.
   - Gradually whisk in the milk and heavy cream, stirring constantly to prevent lumps.
   - Add the dried thyme, salt, and pepper. Continue to cook, stirring occasionally, until the sauce thickens slightly, about 5-7 minutes.
4. **Layer the potatoes:**
   - Arrange half of the sliced potatoes in the prepared baking dish, overlapping slightly.
   - Pour half of the sauce over the potatoes, spreading it evenly with a spoon or spatula.
   - Sprinkle half of the shredded Gruyère cheese and Parmesan cheese over the sauce.
5. **Repeat the layers:**
   - Arrange the remaining sliced potatoes on top.
   - Pour the remaining sauce over the potatoes, spreading it evenly.
   - Sprinkle the remaining shredded Gruyère cheese and Parmesan cheese on top.
6. **Bake:**

- Cover the baking dish with aluminum foil and bake in the preheated oven for 45 minutes.
- Remove the foil and bake for an additional 15-20 minutes, or until the potatoes are tender and the top is golden brown and bubbly.

7. **Serve:**
    - Remove the Scalloped Potatoes from the oven and let them rest for 10 minutes before serving.
    - Garnish with chopped fresh parsley, if desired, for a pop of color.

Scalloped Potatoes are creamy, cheesy, and comforting—a perfect side dish for Christmas dinner or any special occasion. They pair well with roasted meats, poultry, or even as a main dish for vegetarians. Enjoy this decadent and delicious dish with your loved ones!

Spinach and Artichoke Dip

Ingredients:

- 1 (10-ounce) package frozen chopped spinach, thawed and drained
- 1 (14-ounce) can artichoke hearts, drained and chopped
- 1 cup grated Parmesan cheese
- 1 cup shredded mozzarella cheese
- 1 cup mayonnaise
- 1 cup sour cream
- 1/2 cup cream cheese, softened
- 2 cloves garlic, minced
- 1/2 teaspoon salt
- 1/4 teaspoon black pepper
- 1/4 teaspoon red pepper flakes (optional, for a bit of heat)
- 1/4 cup grated Parmesan cheese, for topping
- Fresh parsley, chopped, for garnish (optional)
- Tortilla chips, bread slices, or vegetables, for serving

Instructions:

1. **Preheat the oven:** Preheat your oven to 375°F (190°C). Lightly grease a baking dish (such as an 8x8-inch or similar size).
2. **Prepare the spinach and artichokes:**
    - Thaw the frozen chopped spinach according to package instructions. Squeeze out any excess water from the spinach.
    - Drain the canned artichoke hearts and chop them into smaller pieces.
3. **Mix the dip ingredients:**
    - In a large mixing bowl, combine the drained spinach, chopped artichoke hearts, grated Parmesan cheese, shredded mozzarella cheese, mayonnaise, sour cream, softened cream cheese, minced garlic, salt, black pepper, and optional red pepper flakes. Stir well until all ingredients are thoroughly combined.
4. **Bake the dip:**
    - Transfer the spinach and artichoke mixture to the prepared baking dish, spreading it out evenly.
    - Sprinkle the remaining 1/4 cup of grated Parmesan cheese over the top of the dip.
5. **Bake in the oven:**
    - Bake in the preheated oven for 25-30 minutes, or until the dip is hot and bubbly, and the top is golden brown.
6. **Garnish and serve:**
    - Remove the Spinach and Artichoke Dip from the oven and let it cool for a few minutes.
    - Garnish with chopped fresh parsley, if desired, for a pop of color.
    - Serve warm with tortilla chips, bread slices, or fresh vegetables for dipping.

This Spinach and Artichoke Dip recipe is creamy, cheesy, and packed with flavor—a crowd-pleasing appetizer that's sure to be a hit at your Christmas gathering. Enjoy this delicious dip with friends and family!

Maple Roasted Vegetables

Ingredients:

- 1 pound carrots, peeled and cut into sticks or rounds
- 1 pound sweet potatoes, peeled and cut into cubes
- 1 pound Brussels sprouts, trimmed and halved
- 1 red onion, cut into wedges
- 3 tablespoons olive oil
- 1/4 cup pure maple syrup
- 2 tablespoons balsamic vinegar
- 1 teaspoon Dijon mustard
- 2 cloves garlic, minced
- 1 teaspoon dried thyme
- Salt and pepper, to taste
- Fresh parsley or thyme, chopped (optional, for garnish)

Instructions:

1. **Preheat the oven:** Preheat your oven to 400°F (200°C). Line a large baking sheet with parchment paper or foil.
2. **Prepare the vegetables:**
   - In a large bowl, combine the carrots, sweet potatoes, Brussels sprouts, and red onion wedges.
3. **Make the maple glaze:**
   - In a small bowl, whisk together the olive oil, maple syrup, balsamic vinegar, Dijon mustard, minced garlic, dried thyme, salt, and pepper.
4. **Coat the vegetables:**
   - Pour the maple glaze over the vegetables in the bowl. Toss well to coat all the vegetables evenly with the glaze.
5. **Roast the vegetables:**
   - Spread the coated vegetables in a single layer on the prepared baking sheet.
   - Roast in the preheated oven for 30-35 minutes, stirring halfway through, until the vegetables are tender and caramelized.
6. **Garnish and serve:**
   - Remove the Maple Roasted Vegetables from the oven.
   - Garnish with chopped fresh parsley or thyme, if desired, for added freshness and color.
7. **Enjoy:**
   - Serve the Maple Roasted Vegetables warm as a delicious and festive side dish for your Christmas dinner.

These Maple Roasted Vegetables are flavorful, with a perfect balance of sweetness from the maple syrup and savory notes from the balsamic vinegar and Dijon mustard. They complement roasted meats or poultry beautifully and add a festive touch to your holiday meal. Enjoy this delightful dish with your loved ones!

Caprese Salad

Ingredients:

- 4-5 ripe tomatoes, preferably heirloom or vine-ripened
- 1 pound fresh mozzarella cheese, sliced into rounds or balls
- Fresh basil leaves
- Extra virgin olive oil
- Balsamic glaze or balsamic vinegar (optional)
- Salt and pepper, to taste

Instructions:

1. **Prepare the tomatoes:**
    - Wash the tomatoes thoroughly and slice them into 1/4-inch thick rounds.
2. **Slice the mozzarella:**
    - Slice the fresh mozzarella cheese into rounds of similar thickness to the tomatoes. If using mozzarella balls, you can halve or quarter them.
3. **Assemble the salad:**
    - Arrange the tomato and mozzarella slices alternately on a serving platter or individual plates, overlapping slightly.
4. **Add basil leaves:**
    - Place fresh basil leaves on top of each tomato and mozzarella slice. You can use whole leaves or chiffonade (thinly sliced).
5. **Drizzle with olive oil:**
    - Drizzle extra virgin olive oil generously over the salad.
6. **Season with salt and pepper:**
    - Sprinkle salt and freshly ground black pepper over the salad to taste.
7. **Optional: Add balsamic glaze or vinegar:**
    - For an extra layer of flavor, drizzle balsamic glaze or balsamic vinegar over the salad.
8. **Serve:**
    - Serve the Caprese Salad immediately, garnished with additional basil leaves if desired.

Caprese Salad is best enjoyed fresh, showcasing the vibrant colors and flavors of ripe tomatoes, creamy mozzarella, and fragrant basil. It's a light and refreshing salad that makes a beautiful and delicious addition to your Christmas dinner. Enjoy this classic Italian dish with friends and family!

Herb Crusted Rack of Lamb

Ingredients:

- 2 racks of lamb, about 1 1/2 pounds each (French trimmed if possible)
- Salt and freshly ground black pepper
- 2 tablespoons Dijon mustard
- 2 cloves garlic, minced
- 2 tablespoons fresh rosemary, finely chopped
- 2 tablespoons fresh thyme leaves, finely chopped
- 1/2 cup breadcrumbs (panko or regular)
- 2 tablespoons olive oil
- 2 tablespoons butter

Instructions:

1. **Preheat the oven:** Preheat your oven to 400°F (200°C).
2. **Prepare the lamb:**
   - Pat the racks of lamb dry with paper towels. Season generously with salt and pepper.
3. **Apply Dijon mustard:**
   - In a small bowl, mix together the Dijon mustard and minced garlic. Brush the mustard mixture evenly over the lamb racks.
4. **Make the herb crust:**
   - In another bowl, combine the chopped rosemary, chopped thyme, breadcrumbs, and olive oil. Mix until well combined.
5. **Coat the lamb with herb crust:**
   - Press the herb breadcrumb mixture evenly onto the mustard-coated lamb racks, covering the top and sides.
6. **Sear the lamb:**
   - Heat a large oven-safe skillet or cast iron pan over medium-high heat. Add the butter and heat until melted and foamy.
   - Place the lamb racks, meat-side down, in the skillet. Sear for 2-3 minutes until browned and crispy.
7. **Roast the lamb:**
   - Transfer the skillet to the preheated oven. Roast for 15-20 minutes for medium-rare, or until an instant-read thermometer inserted into the thickest part of the meat registers 125°F (52°C).
8. **Rest and slice:**
   - Remove the lamb from the oven and transfer it to a cutting board. Cover loosely with foil and let it rest for 10 minutes before slicing.
9. **Serve:**
   - Slice the herb-crusted rack of lamb between the bones into individual chops. Arrange on a serving platter and serve immediately.

This herb-crusted rack of lamb is tender, flavorful, and beautifully complemented by the savory herb crust. It's sure to impress your guests and make your Christmas dinner memorable. Serve with roasted vegetables, potatoes, or a side salad for a complete holiday meal. Enjoy!

Mushroom Risotto

Ingredients:

- 1 1/2 cups Arborio rice
- 6 cups vegetable or chicken broth (homemade or low-sodium)
- 1/2 ounce dried porcini mushrooms
- 2 tablespoons olive oil
- 2 tablespoons unsalted butter
- 1 small onion, finely chopped
- 3 cloves garlic, minced
- 1 pound fresh mushrooms (such as cremini or button), sliced
- 1/2 cup dry white wine (optional)
- 1/2 cup grated Parmesan cheese
- Salt and pepper, to taste
- Fresh parsley, chopped, for garnish

Instructions:

1. **Prepare the broth:**
    - In a saucepan, bring the vegetable or chicken broth to a simmer. Add the dried porcini mushrooms to the broth and let them rehydrate for about 10 minutes. Once rehydrated, remove the porcini mushrooms with a slotted spoon, chop them finely, and set them aside. Keep the broth warm over low heat.
2. **Sauté the onions and garlic:**
    - In a large, heavy-bottomed pot or Dutch oven, heat the olive oil and butter over medium heat. Add the chopped onion and cook for 3-4 minutes until softened. Add the minced garlic and cook for another 1-2 minutes until fragrant.
3. **Cook the fresh mushrooms:**
    - Add the sliced fresh mushrooms and chopped rehydrated porcini mushrooms to the pot. Cook for 5-6 minutes, stirring occasionally, until the mushrooms are golden brown and any liquid released has evaporated.
4. **Toast the rice:**
    - Add the Arborio rice to the pot with the mushrooms. Cook, stirring constantly, for 1-2 minutes until the rice is well-coated with oil and slightly toasted.
5. **Deglaze with wine (optional):**
    - If using, pour in the dry white wine. Stir constantly until the wine has been absorbed by the rice.
6. **Add the broth:**
    - Ladle in one cup of warm broth into the rice mixture. Stir constantly until the broth is absorbed. Repeat this process, adding one cup of broth at a time and stirring frequently, allowing each addition to be absorbed before adding more. This process will take about 20-25 minutes. The rice should be tender but still slightly firm (al dente) when done.
7. **Finish the risotto:**

- Stir in the grated Parmesan cheese until melted and well combined. Season with salt and pepper to taste.
8. **Serve:**
    - Remove the mushroom risotto from heat. Serve warm, garnished with chopped fresh parsley.

Mushroom risotto is creamy, flavorful, and luxurious—a perfect dish to impress your guests at Christmas dinner. It pairs well with roasted meats, poultry, or can be enjoyed on its own as a hearty vegetarian main course. Enjoy this comforting Italian classic with your loved ones!

Crab Cakes

Ingredients:

- 1 pound lump crabmeat, picked over for shells
- 1/2 cup breadcrumbs (panko or regular)
- 1/4 cup mayonnaise
- 1 large egg, lightly beaten
- 2 tablespoons chopped fresh parsley
- 1 tablespoon Dijon mustard
- 1 tablespoon Worcestershire sauce
- 1 teaspoon Old Bay seasoning (or more to taste)
- 1/4 teaspoon salt
- 1/4 teaspoon black pepper
- 1/4 cup finely chopped green onions (green parts only)
- 2 tablespoons unsalted butter
- 2 tablespoons olive oil
- Lemon wedges, for serving
- Tartar sauce or remoulade sauce, for serving (optional)

Instructions:

1. **Prepare the crab cakes:**
    - In a large mixing bowl, gently combine the lump crabmeat, breadcrumbs, mayonnaise, beaten egg, chopped parsley, Dijon mustard, Worcestershire sauce, Old Bay seasoning, salt, pepper, and chopped green onions. Be careful not to break up the crabmeat too much; you want the cakes to be lumpy with crab chunks.
2. **Form the crab cakes:**
    - Divide the mixture into 8 equal portions and shape each portion into a patty, about 1 inch thick. Place the formed crab cakes on a baking sheet lined with parchment paper. Refrigerate for at least 30 minutes to help them firm up.
3. **Cook the crab cakes:**
    - In a large skillet, heat the butter and olive oil over medium-high heat until the butter is melted and bubbly.
    - Carefully place the crab cakes in the skillet (you may need to do this in batches to avoid overcrowding). Cook for about 4-5 minutes on each side, or until golden brown and heated through. Use a spatula to carefully flip them halfway through cooking.
4. **Serve:**
    - Transfer the cooked crab cakes to a serving platter. Serve warm with lemon wedges and your choice of tartar sauce or remoulade sauce on the side, if desired.
5. **Enjoy:**

- Crab cakes are best enjoyed immediately while they are still warm and crispy on the outside, with tender, flavorful crabmeat inside.

Crab cakes are a delightful treat that can be enjoyed as an appetizer or served with a side salad or vegetables for a main course. They are sure to impress your guests with their delicious flavor and elegant presentation at your Christmas dinner!

Quinoa Salad with Roasted Vegetables

Ingredients:

- 1 cup quinoa
- 2 cups water or vegetable broth
- 1 medium sweet potato, peeled and diced
- 1 red bell pepper, diced
- 1 zucchini, diced
- 1 yellow squash, diced
- 1 red onion, thinly sliced
- 3 tablespoons olive oil
- Salt and pepper, to taste
- 1 teaspoon smoked paprika (optional)
- 1/2 cup chopped fresh parsley or cilantro
- 1/4 cup toasted pine nuts or chopped almonds (optional)
- Juice of 1 lemon
- Zest of 1 lemon

For the dressing:

- 1/4 cup extra virgin olive oil
- 2 tablespoons balsamic vinegar or red wine vinegar
- 1 tablespoon Dijon mustard
- 1 clove garlic, minced
- Salt and pepper, to taste

Instructions:

1. **Prepare the quinoa:**
    - Rinse the quinoa under cold water using a fine-mesh sieve. In a saucepan, bring the quinoa and water or vegetable broth to a boil. Reduce heat to low, cover, and simmer for 15-20 minutes, or until the liquid is absorbed and the quinoa is cooked. Fluff with a fork and let it cool slightly.
2. **Roast the vegetables:**
    - Preheat your oven to 400°F (200°C).
    - Place the diced sweet potato, red bell pepper, zucchini, yellow squash, and red onion on a large baking sheet. Drizzle with olive oil and season with salt, pepper, and smoked paprika, if using. Toss to coat evenly.
    - Roast in the preheated oven for 20-25 minutes, or until the vegetables are tender and slightly caramelized. Stir halfway through cooking for even roasting.
3. **Make the dressing:**
    - In a small bowl, whisk together the extra virgin olive oil, balsamic vinegar, Dijon mustard, minced garlic, salt, and pepper until well combined.
4. **Assemble the salad:**

- In a large bowl, combine the cooked quinoa, roasted vegetables, chopped parsley or cilantro, and toasted pine nuts or chopped almonds, if using.
- Pour the dressing over the salad and toss gently to combine. Add more salt and pepper to taste, if needed.
5. **Add lemon zest and juice:**
    - Add the juice of 1 lemon and the zest of 1 lemon to the salad. Toss again gently to incorporate the flavors.
6. **Serve:**
    - Transfer the Quinoa Salad with Roasted Vegetables to a serving platter or bowl. Serve warm or at room temperature as a nutritious and satisfying dish for Christmas dinner.

This Quinoa Salad with Roasted Vegetables is packed with flavor, textures, and nutrients, making it a perfect addition to your holiday feast. It can be served as a main course for vegetarians or as a hearty side dish alongside grilled meats or fish. Enjoy the vibrant colors and delicious flavors of this wholesome salad!

Roasted Beet Salad with Goat Cheese

Ingredients:

- 4 medium-sized beets (red or golden), trimmed and scrubbed
- 4 ounces goat cheese (chevre), crumbled
- 1/4 cup walnuts or pecans, toasted and chopped
- 4 cups mixed salad greens (arugula, baby spinach, or mixed greens)
- 2 tablespoons extra virgin olive oil
- 1 tablespoon balsamic vinegar
- 1 teaspoon honey
- Salt and pepper, to taste
- Fresh herbs (such as parsley or thyme), for garnish (optional)

Instructions:

1. **Roast the beets:**
    - Preheat your oven to 400°F (200°C).
    - Place the scrubbed and trimmed beets on a large piece of aluminum foil. Drizzle with a little olive oil and season with salt and pepper. Wrap the beets in the foil, creating a sealed packet.
    - Roast in the preheated oven for 45-60 minutes, or until the beets are tender when pierced with a fork. Cooking time will depend on the size of the beets. Let the beets cool slightly.
2. **Prepare the salad greens:**
    - While the beets are roasting, wash and dry the mixed salad greens. Place them in a large salad bowl.
3. **Make the dressing:**
    - In a small bowl, whisk together the extra virgin olive oil, balsamic vinegar, honey, salt, and pepper until well combined.
4. **Assemble the salad:**
    - Once the beets are cool enough to handle, peel off the skin using your fingers or a small knife (it should come off easily). Cut the beets into wedges or slices.
    - Arrange the roasted beet slices on top of the mixed salad greens in the salad bowl.
    - Drizzle the dressing over the salad and gently toss to coat the greens and beets evenly with the dressing.
5. **Add goat cheese and nuts:**
    - Sprinkle the crumbled goat cheese and toasted chopped nuts (walnuts or pecans) over the salad.
6. **Garnish and serve:**
    - Garnish the Roasted Beet Salad with Goat Cheese with fresh herbs, if desired.
    - Serve immediately as a colorful and flavorful salad option for Christmas dinner.

This Roasted Beet Salad with Goat Cheese combines earthy roasted beets with creamy goat cheese, crunchy nuts, and a tangy-sweet dressing, creating a delightful balance of flavors and textures. It's a perfect salad to complement holiday dishes and impress your guests with its vibrant presentation. Enjoy this nutritious and delicious salad!

Chicken Piccata

Ingredients:

- 4 boneless, skinless chicken breasts (about 1 1/2 pounds total)
- Salt and pepper, to taste
- 1/2 cup all-purpose flour
- 4 tablespoons unsalted butter, divided
- 2 tablespoons olive oil
- 1/2 cup chicken broth
- 1/4 cup fresh lemon juice (about 2 lemons)
- 1/4 cup capers, drained
- 1/4 cup chopped fresh parsley, for garnish
- Lemon slices, for garnish

Instructions:

1. **Prepare the chicken:**
   - Place each chicken breast between two sheets of plastic wrap or parchment paper. Use a meat mallet or rolling pin to pound the chicken breasts to an even thickness of about 1/2 inch. Season both sides with salt and pepper.
2. **Dredge the chicken:**
   - In a shallow dish, place the flour. Dredge each chicken breast in the flour, shaking off any excess.
3. **Cook the chicken:**
   - In a large skillet, heat 2 tablespoons of butter and 2 tablespoons of olive oil over medium-high heat until the butter is melted and bubbly.
   - Add the chicken breasts to the skillet and cook for about 3-4 minutes per side, or until golden brown and cooked through. Remove the chicken from the skillet and transfer to a plate.
4. **Make the sauce:**
   - In the same skillet, add the chicken broth, lemon juice, and capers. Scrape up any browned bits from the bottom of the skillet with a wooden spoon.
   - Bring the sauce to a simmer and cook for about 2-3 minutes, allowing it to reduce slightly.
5. **Finish the dish:**
   - Stir in the remaining 2 tablespoons of butter until melted and the sauce is smooth and slightly thickened.
   - Return the chicken breasts to the skillet, turning them in the sauce to coat evenly. Cook for another 1-2 minutes to heat through.
6. **Garnish and serve:**
   - Remove the skillet from heat. Garnish the Chicken Piccata with chopped fresh parsley and lemon slices.
   - Serve the chicken breasts warm, spooning the sauce and capers over the top.

Chicken Piccata pairs well with pasta, rice, or mashed potatoes, making it a versatile main course for your Christmas dinner. Its bright, tangy flavors from the lemon and capers are sure to delight your guests. Enjoy this delicious Italian classic with family and friends!

Pecan Crusted Salmon

Ingredients:

- 4 salmon fillets, skin-on or skinless (about 6 ounces each)
- Salt and pepper, to taste
- 1 cup pecans, finely chopped or ground
- 1/4 cup panko breadcrumbs (optional, for added crunch)
- 2 tablespoons Dijon mustard
- 2 tablespoons maple syrup
- 1 tablespoon olive oil
- 1 tablespoon fresh lemon juice
- 1 teaspoon paprika
- 1/2 teaspoon garlic powder
- Fresh parsley, chopped, for garnish (optional)
- Lemon wedges, for serving

Instructions:

1. **Prepare the salmon:**
   - Preheat your oven to 400°F (200°C). Line a baking sheet with parchment paper or lightly grease it with olive oil.
   - Pat the salmon fillets dry with paper towels. Season both sides with salt and pepper.
2. **Make the pecan crust:**
   - In a shallow dish, combine the finely chopped or ground pecans, panko breadcrumbs (if using), paprika, and garlic powder. Mix well.
3. **Coat the salmon:**
   - In another small bowl, whisk together the Dijon mustard, maple syrup, olive oil, and fresh lemon juice.
   - Brush the mustard mixture evenly over the top and sides of each salmon fillet.
4. **Apply the pecan crust:**
   - Press the pecan mixture firmly onto the top of each salmon fillet, coating it generously and evenly.
5. **Bake the salmon:**
   - Place the coated salmon fillets onto the prepared baking sheet.
   - Bake in the preheated oven for 12-15 minutes, depending on the thickness of the fillets, or until the salmon flakes easily with a fork and the pecan crust is golden brown and crispy.
6. **Serve:**
   - Remove the Pecan Crusted Salmon from the oven and let it rest for a few minutes.
   - Garnish with chopped fresh parsley, if desired, and serve warm with lemon wedges on the side.

Pecan Crusted Salmon is a delicious and elegant dish that's perfect for Christmas dinner. The combination of crunchy pecans, tangy Dijon mustard, and sweet maple syrup complements the richness of the salmon beautifully. Serve it with roasted vegetables or a side salad for a complete holiday meal. Enjoy this flavorful and nutritious salmon dish with your loved ones!

Eggplant Parmesan

Ingredients:

- 2 large eggplants, sliced into 1/2-inch rounds
- Salt, for sprinkling
- 1 cup all-purpose flour
- 4 large eggs, beaten
- 2 cups breadcrumbs (panko or regular)
- 1 cup grated Parmesan cheese, divided
- 1/4 cup chopped fresh basil or parsley
- 4 cups marinara sauce (homemade or store-bought)
- 1 pound fresh mozzarella cheese, sliced
- Olive oil, for frying
- Fresh basil leaves, for garnish (optional)

Instructions:

1. **Prepare the eggplant:**
    - Place the eggplant slices on a baking sheet or large platter. Sprinkle both sides generously with salt and let them sit for about 30 minutes. This helps to draw out excess moisture and bitterness from the eggplant. After 30 minutes, pat dry with paper towels.
2. **Bread the eggplant:**
    - Set up a breading station with three shallow dishes: one with flour, one with beaten eggs, and one with breadcrumbs mixed with half of the grated Parmesan cheese and chopped fresh basil or parsley.
    - Dredge each eggplant slice in the flour, shaking off any excess. Dip into the beaten eggs, letting any excess drip off. Finally, coat evenly with the breadcrumb mixture, pressing gently to adhere. Place breaded eggplant slices on a baking sheet.
3. **Fry the eggplant:**
    - In a large skillet, heat olive oil over medium heat. Working in batches, fry the breaded eggplant slices for 2-3 minutes per side, or until golden brown and crispy. Transfer to a paper towel-lined plate to drain excess oil.
4. **Assemble the Eggplant Parmesan:**
    - Preheat your oven to 375°F (190°C).
    - Spread a thin layer of marinara sauce on the bottom of a large baking dish.
    - Arrange a layer of fried eggplant slices on top of the sauce, slightly overlapping. Spoon more marinara sauce over the eggplant slices, followed by slices of fresh mozzarella cheese. Sprinkle with some of the remaining grated Parmesan cheese. Repeat the layers, finishing with a layer of marinara sauce and mozzarella cheese on top.
5. **Bake the Eggplant Parmesan:**

- Cover the baking dish loosely with aluminum foil. Bake in the preheated oven for 25-30 minutes, or until the sauce is bubbling and the cheese is melted and slightly golden.

6. **Serve:**
    - Remove the Eggplant Parmesan from the oven. Let it rest for 5-10 minutes before serving. Garnish with fresh basil leaves, if desired.

Eggplant Parmesan is best served warm, accompanied by a side of pasta or a green salad. It's a delicious and satisfying vegetarian dish that will impress your guests at Christmas dinner with its layers of flavors and comforting textures. Enjoy this Italian classic with family and friends!

Wild Rice Pilaf

Ingredients:

- 1 cup wild rice
- 1/2 cup long-grain white rice
- 2 tablespoons olive oil or butter
- 1 small onion, finely chopped
- 2 cloves garlic, minced
- 1 celery stalk, finely chopped
- 1 carrot, finely chopped
- 1/2 cup sliced mushrooms (optional)
- 3 cups chicken or vegetable broth
- 1/4 cup chopped fresh parsley
- 1/4 cup chopped almonds or pecans (optional)
- Salt and pepper, to taste

Instructions:

1. **Rinse and cook the wild rice:**
    - Rinse the wild rice under cold water using a fine-mesh sieve. In a medium saucepan, bring 2 cups of water to a boil. Add the rinsed wild rice, reduce heat to low, cover, and simmer for 40-45 minutes, or until the wild rice is tender and has popped open. Drain any excess water and set aside.
2. **Cook the white rice:**
    - In another saucepan, rinse the white rice under cold water and cook according to package instructions using 1 cup of water. Once cooked, fluff with a fork and set aside.
3. **Sauté the vegetables:**
    - In a large skillet or sauté pan, heat olive oil or melt butter over medium heat. Add the chopped onion and cook for 2-3 minutes until translucent.
    - Add the minced garlic, celery, carrot, and sliced mushrooms (if using). Cook for another 5-6 minutes, stirring occasionally, until the vegetables are tender.
4. **Combine the rice and vegetables:**
    - Add the cooked wild rice and white rice to the skillet with the sautéed vegetables. Mix well to combine.
5. **Add the broth:**
    - Pour in the chicken or vegetable broth. Bring to a simmer over medium heat. Reduce heat to low, cover, and cook for 15-20 minutes, or until the liquid is absorbed and the rice is tender.
6. **Finish and garnish:**
    - Stir in the chopped fresh parsley and chopped almonds or pecans (if using). Season with salt and pepper to taste.
7. **Serve:**

- Transfer the Wild Rice Pilaf to a serving dish or bowl. Garnish with additional parsley or nuts, if desired. Serve warm as a delicious side dish for Christmas dinner.

Wild Rice Pilaf is hearty, aromatic, and pairs well with roasted meats, poultry, or as a standalone vegetarian dish. It adds a festive touch to your holiday table with its rich flavors and nutritious ingredients. Enjoy this comforting and flavorful pilaf with your loved ones!

Antipasto Platter

Ingredients:

- Assorted cured meats (such as prosciutto, salami, coppa, or mortadella)
- Assorted cheeses (such as mozzarella balls, provolone, or aged Parmesan)
- Marinated vegetables (such as artichoke hearts, roasted red peppers, or sun-dried tomatoes)
- Olives (such as Kalamata or green olives)
- Fresh vegetables (such as cherry tomatoes, cucumber slices, or bell pepper strips)
- Breadsticks or slices of crusty bread
- Fresh herbs (such as basil or parsley) for garnish
- Extra virgin olive oil and balsamic vinegar, for drizzling (optional)
- Fig jam or honey, for serving (optional)

Instructions:

1. **Prepare the meats and cheeses:**
   - Arrange a selection of cured meats and cheeses on a large serving platter or wooden board. Fold or roll the slices of meats like prosciutto or salami for an attractive presentation. Place chunks or slices of cheeses around the platter.
2. **Arrange the marinated vegetables and olives:**
   - Place marinated vegetables, such as artichoke hearts, roasted red peppers, or sun-dried tomatoes, in small piles or clusters on the platter. Scatter olives around the platter for variety.
3. **Add fresh vegetables and bread:**
   - Arrange fresh vegetables like cherry tomatoes, cucumber slices, or bell pepper strips in between the meats and cheeses. Place breadsticks or slices of crusty bread in a basket or on the platter.
4. **Garnish and serve:**
   - Garnish the Antipasto Platter with fresh herbs, such as basil or parsley, for a pop of color. Optionally, drizzle extra virgin olive oil and balsamic vinegar over the vegetables and meats for added flavor.
   - Serve the Antipasto Platter with small bowls of fig jam or honey on the side for dipping or spreading on bread.
5. **Enjoy:**
   - Serve the Antipasto Platter as a festive and delicious appetizer before your Christmas dinner. Your guests can nibble on a variety of flavors and textures, creating a delightful start to the meal.

An Antipasto Platter not only looks impressive but also offers a variety of tastes that everyone can enjoy. It's a perfect addition to your holiday spread, allowing guests to sample a range of Italian flavors in one appetizing display.

Pear and Gorgonzola Salad

Ingredients:

- 6 cups mixed salad greens (such as baby spinach, arugula, or mixed greens)
- 2 ripe pears, thinly sliced (choose varieties like Bartlett or Anjou)
- 1/2 cup crumbled Gorgonzola cheese
- 1/2 cup walnuts or pecans, toasted and roughly chopped
- 1/4 cup dried cranberries or fresh pomegranate arils (optional, for added sweetness)

For the vinaigrette:

- 1/4 cup extra virgin olive oil
- 2 tablespoons balsamic vinegar
- 1 tablespoon honey or maple syrup
- 1 teaspoon Dijon mustard
- Salt and freshly ground black pepper, to taste

Instructions:

1. **Prepare the salad greens:**
    - In a large salad bowl, toss together the mixed salad greens.
2. **Toast the nuts (if not toasted):**
    - In a dry skillet over medium heat, toast the walnuts or pecans for a few minutes until lightly golden and fragrant. Remove from heat and let them cool slightly before chopping.
3. **Make the vinaigrette:**
    - In a small bowl or jar, whisk together the extra virgin olive oil, balsamic vinegar, honey or maple syrup, Dijon mustard, salt, and pepper until well combined. Adjust sweetness and tanginess to your liking by adding more honey or vinegar, if necessary.
4. **Assemble the salad:**
    - Add the sliced pears, crumbled Gorgonzola cheese, toasted nuts, and dried cranberries or pomegranate arils (if using) to the bowl with the mixed greens.
5. **Drizzle with vinaigrette:**
    - Pour the vinaigrette over the salad ingredients. Gently toss the salad to coat evenly with the dressing.
6. **Serve:**
    - Transfer the Pear and Gorgonzola Salad to a serving platter or individual salad plates. Serve immediately as a refreshing and flavorful salad for Christmas dinner.

This Pear and Gorgonzola Salad combines sweet and savory flavors with a delightful crunch from the nuts, making it a perfect complement to holiday dishes. It's light yet satisfying, adding a burst of freshness to your festive table. Enjoy this delicious salad with family and friends during your holiday celebration!

Vegetarian Stuffed Peppers

Ingredients:

- 4 large bell peppers (any color), tops cut off and seeds removed
- 1 cup quinoa, rinsed
- 2 cups vegetable broth or water
- 1 tablespoon olive oil
- 1 small onion, finely chopped
- 2 cloves garlic, minced
- 1 medium zucchini, diced
- 1 cup diced tomatoes (fresh or canned)
- 1 cup canned black beans, drained and rinsed
- 1 teaspoon ground cumin
- 1 teaspoon paprika
- 1/2 teaspoon chili powder (optional, for heat)
- Salt and pepper, to taste
- 1 cup shredded cheese (such as cheddar or mozzarella), divided
- Fresh parsley or cilantro, chopped, for garnish (optional)

Instructions:

1. **Prepare the quinoa:**
   - In a medium saucepan, bring the vegetable broth or water to a boil. Add the rinsed quinoa, reduce heat to low, cover, and simmer for 15-20 minutes, or until the liquid is absorbed and the quinoa is cooked. Fluff with a fork and set aside.
2. **Preheat the oven:**
   - Preheat your oven to 375°F (190°C).
3. **Prepare the bell peppers:**
   - Place the hollowed-out bell peppers upright in a baking dish. If needed, trim the bottoms slightly to help them stand upright.
4. **Make the filling:**
   - In a large skillet, heat olive oil over medium heat. Add the chopped onion and cook for 2-3 minutes until softened.
   - Add the minced garlic and diced zucchini to the skillet. Cook for another 3-4 minutes, stirring occasionally, until the zucchini begins to soften.
   - Stir in the diced tomatoes, black beans, ground cumin, paprika, and chili powder (if using). Season with salt and pepper to taste. Cook for 2-3 minutes to combine flavors.
5. **Combine the filling:**
   - Remove the skillet from heat. Stir in the cooked quinoa and half of the shredded cheese until well combined. Adjust seasoning if needed.
6. **Stuff the peppers:**
   - Spoon the quinoa and vegetable mixture evenly into the hollowed-out bell peppers, pressing gently to pack the filling.

7. **Bake the stuffed peppers:**
    - Sprinkle the remaining shredded cheese over the tops of the stuffed peppers.
    - Cover the baking dish loosely with aluminum foil. Bake in the preheated oven for 25-30 minutes, or until the peppers are tender and the cheese is melted and bubbly.
8. **Serve:**
    - Remove the Vegetarian Stuffed Peppers from the oven. Garnish with chopped fresh parsley or cilantro, if desired.
    - Serve the stuffed peppers warm as a delicious and satisfying vegetarian main course for Christmas dinner.

These Vegetarian Stuffed Peppers are packed with protein from the quinoa and black beans, and they are full of flavor with the spices and vegetables. They make a colorful addition to your holiday table and will satisfy vegetarians and meat-eaters alike. Enjoy this wholesome dish with your loved ones during your festive celebration!

Cauliflower Gratin

Ingredients:

- 1 large head of cauliflower, cut into florets
- 2 tablespoons butter
- 2 tablespoons all-purpose flour
- 1 1/2 cups milk (preferably whole milk)
- 1 cup shredded Gruyère cheese (or Swiss cheese), divided
- 1/2 cup grated Parmesan cheese
- 1/2 teaspoon salt, or to taste
- 1/4 teaspoon black pepper, or to taste
- 1/4 teaspoon ground nutmeg (optional)
- 1/2 cup breadcrumbs (panko or regular)
- Fresh parsley, chopped, for garnish (optional)

Instructions:

1. **Preheat the oven:**
   - Preheat your oven to 375°F (190°C). Lightly grease a baking dish with butter or cooking spray.
2. **Prepare the cauliflower:**
   - Bring a large pot of salted water to a boil. Add the cauliflower florets and cook for about 5 minutes, or until just tender. Drain well and set aside.
3. **Make the cheese sauce:**
   - In a medium saucepan, melt the butter over medium heat. Stir in the flour and cook for 1-2 minutes, stirring constantly, until smooth and bubbly.
   - Gradually whisk in the milk, stirring constantly to avoid lumps. Cook for 5-7 minutes, or until the sauce thickens and coats the back of a spoon.
   - Remove the saucepan from heat. Stir in 3/4 cup of shredded Gruyère cheese (or Swiss cheese) and the grated Parmesan cheese until melted and smooth. Season with salt, pepper, and nutmeg (if using). Adjust seasoning to taste.
4. **Assemble the gratin:**
   - Arrange the blanched cauliflower florets in the prepared baking dish in an even layer.
   - Pour the cheese sauce evenly over the cauliflower, making sure to coat all the florets.
5. **Top with breadcrumbs and cheese:**
   - In a small bowl, combine the remaining 1/4 cup of shredded Gruyère cheese with the breadcrumbs. Sprinkle this mixture evenly over the top of the cauliflower and cheese sauce.
6. **Bake the gratin:**
   - Cover the baking dish loosely with aluminum foil to prevent excessive browning. Bake in the preheated oven for 25-30 minutes.

- Remove the foil and continue baking for an additional 10-15 minutes, or until the top is golden brown and bubbly.
7. **Serve:**
    - Remove the Cauliflower Gratin from the oven and let it cool slightly before serving.
    - Garnish with chopped fresh parsley, if desired, and serve warm as a delicious side dish for Christmas dinner.

Cauliflower Gratin is creamy, cheesy, and full of flavor, making it a comforting and satisfying addition to your holiday meal. Enjoy this delicious dish with your family and friends during your festive celebration!

Apple Cranberry Walnut Salad

Ingredients:

- 6 cups mixed salad greens (such as baby spinach, arugula, or mixed greens)
- 2 medium apples (such as Granny Smith or Honeycrisp), cored and thinly sliced
- 1/2 cup dried cranberries
- 1/2 cup walnuts, toasted and roughly chopped
- 1/2 cup crumbled feta or goat cheese (optional)
- Fresh parsley or mint leaves, chopped, for garnish (optional)

For the vinaigrette:

- 1/4 cup extra virgin olive oil
- 2 tablespoons apple cider vinegar
- 1 tablespoon honey or maple syrup
- 1 teaspoon Dijon mustard
- Salt and freshly ground black pepper, to taste

Instructions:

1. **Prepare the salad greens:**
   - In a large salad bowl, toss together the mixed salad greens.
2. **Toast the walnuts:**
   - In a dry skillet over medium heat, toast the walnuts for a few minutes until lightly golden and fragrant. Remove from heat and let them cool slightly before chopping.
3. **Make the vinaigrette:**
   - In a small bowl or jar, whisk together the extra virgin olive oil, apple cider vinegar, honey or maple syrup, Dijon mustard, salt, and pepper until well combined. Adjust sweetness and tanginess to your liking by adding more honey or vinegar, if necessary.
4. **Assemble the salad:**
   - Add the sliced apples, dried cranberries, toasted walnuts, and crumbled feta or goat cheese (if using) to the bowl with the mixed greens.
5. **Drizzle with vinaigrette:**
   - Pour the vinaigrette over the salad ingredients. Gently toss the salad to coat evenly with the dressing.
6. **Serve:**
   - Transfer the Apple Cranberry Walnut Salad to a serving platter or individual salad plates. Garnish with chopped fresh parsley or mint leaves, if desired.
7. **Enjoy:**
   - Serve the salad immediately as a refreshing and flavorful side dish for Christmas dinner.

This Apple Cranberry Walnut Salad is light yet satisfying, with a perfect balance of sweet, tart, and crunchy elements. It's a colorful addition to your holiday table and pairs beautifully with a variety of main dishes. Enjoy this vibrant and delicious salad with your loved ones during your festive celebration!

Beef Stroganoff

Ingredients:

- 1 lb (450g) beef sirloin or tenderloin, thinly sliced into strips
- Salt and pepper, to taste
- 2 tablespoons olive oil
- 1 onion, finely chopped
- 2 cloves garlic, minced
- 8 oz (225g) mushrooms, sliced
- 2 tablespoons all-purpose flour
- 1 cup beef broth
- 1 tablespoon Worcestershire sauce
- 1 tablespoon Dijon mustard
- 1 cup sour cream
- Fresh parsley, chopped, for garnish
- Cooked egg noodles or rice, for serving

Instructions:

1. **Prepare the beef:**
    - Season the beef strips with salt and pepper.
2. **Sear the beef:**
    - In a large skillet or frying pan, heat 1 tablespoon of olive oil over medium-high heat. Add half of the beef strips and cook for 1-2 minutes per side until browned. Remove the beef from the skillet and set aside. Repeat with the remaining beef strips, adding more oil if necessary.
3. **Cook the onions and mushrooms:**
    - In the same skillet, add the remaining tablespoon of olive oil if needed. Add the chopped onion and cook for 2-3 minutes until softened.
    - Add the minced garlic and sliced mushrooms. Cook for another 4-5 minutes until the mushrooms are browned and softened.
4. **Make the sauce:**
    - Sprinkle the flour over the mushrooms and onions. Stir well to coat evenly and cook for 1 minute.
    - Gradually add the beef broth, stirring constantly to avoid lumps. Bring to a simmer and cook for 2-3 minutes until the sauce thickens.
5. **Finish the sauce:**
    - Stir in the Worcestershire sauce and Dijon mustard. Reduce heat to low.
6. **Add the beef back to the skillet:**
    - Return the cooked beef strips and any juices that have accumulated to the skillet. Stir well to combine with the sauce. Cook for 2-3 minutes until the beef is heated through.
7. **Add the sour cream:**

- Remove the skillet from heat. Stir in the sour cream until well combined. Adjust seasoning with salt and pepper to taste.
8. **Serve:**
    - Serve the Beef Stroganoff hot over cooked egg noodles or rice.
    - Garnish with chopped fresh parsley.

Beef Stroganoff is rich, creamy, and packed with savory flavors, making it a comforting and satisfying dish for Christmas dinner. Enjoy this classic recipe with your family and friends for a festive and delicious holiday meal!

Smoked Gouda Macaroni and Cheese

Ingredients:

- 8 oz (about 2 cups) elbow macaroni or pasta of your choice
- 4 tablespoons unsalted butter
- 1/4 cup all-purpose flour
- 2 cups milk (preferably whole milk)
- 1 cup heavy cream
- 8 oz smoked Gouda cheese, grated
- 4 oz sharp cheddar cheese, grated
- Salt and pepper, to taste
- 1/4 teaspoon paprika (optional, for color)
- 1/4 cup breadcrumbs (panko or regular)
- Fresh parsley, chopped, for garnish (optional)

Instructions:

1. **Cook the pasta:**
   - Cook the elbow macaroni or pasta according to package instructions in a large pot of salted boiling water until al dente. Drain well and set aside.
2. **Make the cheese sauce:**
   - In a large saucepan or Dutch oven, melt the butter over medium heat. Whisk in the flour and cook for 1-2 minutes until smooth and bubbly.
   - Gradually whisk in the milk and heavy cream, stirring constantly to avoid lumps. Cook for 5-7 minutes, or until the mixture thickens and coats the back of a spoon.
3. **Add the cheeses:**
   - Reduce heat to low. Gradually stir in the grated smoked Gouda and sharp cheddar cheese until melted and smooth. Stir in paprika, if using. Season with salt and pepper to taste.
4. **Combine the pasta and cheese sauce:**
   - Add the cooked and drained pasta to the cheese sauce. Stir well until the pasta is evenly coated with the cheese sauce.
5. **Bake the macaroni and cheese:**
   - Preheat your oven to 350°F (175°C). Transfer the macaroni and cheese mixture to a greased baking dish.
   - Sprinkle breadcrumbs evenly over the top of the macaroni and cheese.
6. **Bake for 20-25 minutes:**
   - Bake in the preheated oven for 20-25 minutes, or until the top is golden brown and bubbly.
7. **Serve:**
   - Remove from the oven and let it cool slightly before serving.
   - Garnish with chopped fresh parsley, if desired.

Smoked Gouda Macaroni and Cheese is creamy, cheesy, and has a delicious smoky flavor that adds a unique twist to this classic dish. It's a perfect comfort food to enjoy with family and friends during your Christmas dinner. Enjoy this indulgent and flavorful macaroni and cheese as a delightful addition to your holiday feast!

Chicken Marsala

Ingredients:

- 4 boneless, skinless chicken breasts (about 1.5 lbs), pounded to even thickness
- Salt and pepper, to taste
- 1/2 cup all-purpose flour, for dredging
- 4 tablespoons unsalted butter, divided
- 2 tablespoons olive oil
- 8 oz cremini mushrooms, sliced
- 2 cloves garlic, minced
- 1 cup Marsala wine
- 1 cup chicken broth
- 1/2 cup heavy cream (optional, for a richer sauce)
- Fresh parsley, chopped, for garnish

Instructions:

1. **Prepare the chicken:**
    - Season the chicken breasts with salt and pepper on both sides. Dredge each chicken breast in flour, shaking off any excess.
2. **Cook the chicken:**
    - In a large skillet or frying pan, heat 2 tablespoons of butter and olive oil over medium-high heat. Add the chicken breasts and cook for about 4-5 minutes per side, or until golden brown and cooked through. Remove the chicken from the skillet and set aside.
3. **Sauté the mushrooms and garlic:**
    - In the same skillet, melt the remaining 2 tablespoons of butter. Add the sliced mushrooms and cook for 5-6 minutes, stirring occasionally, until they are browned and softened. Add the minced garlic and cook for another minute until fragrant.
4. **Make the Marsala sauce:**
    - Pour the Marsala wine into the skillet, scraping up any browned bits from the bottom of the pan. Cook for 2-3 minutes, allowing the wine to reduce slightly.
5. **Simmer the sauce:**
    - Stir in the chicken broth and bring the mixture to a simmer. Reduce heat to medium-low and let it simmer for about 10 minutes, or until the sauce has reduced by about half and thickened.
6. **Finish the sauce (optional):**
    - If using heavy cream for a richer sauce, stir it into the skillet and simmer for another 2-3 minutes until heated through.
7. **Add the chicken back to the skillet:**
    - Return the cooked chicken breasts to the skillet, turning them to coat in the sauce. Simmer for a few more minutes to heat the chicken through.
8. **Serve:**

- Garnish the Chicken Marsala with chopped fresh parsley.
- Serve hot over cooked pasta, rice, or mashed potatoes, and spoon extra sauce over the chicken.

Chicken Marsala is savory, flavorful, and pairs beautifully with a variety of side dishes, making it a perfect main course for your Christmas dinner. Enjoy this delicious and comforting Italian-inspired dish with your loved ones during the holiday season!

Baked Stuffed Lobster Tails

Ingredients:

- 4 lobster tails (about 6-8 oz each)
- 4 tablespoons unsalted butter, melted
- 2 cloves garlic, minced
- 1/2 cup breadcrumbs (panko or regular)
- 1/4 cup grated Parmesan cheese
- 2 tablespoons fresh parsley, chopped
- Salt and pepper, to taste
- Lemon wedges, for serving

Instructions:

1. **Prepare the lobster tails:**
   - Preheat your oven to 375°F (190°C). Line a baking sheet with parchment paper or foil.
   - Using kitchen shears or a sharp knife, carefully cut through the top of each lobster tail shell lengthwise, starting from the open end to the tail. Be careful not to cut through the bottom shell or the meat.
   - Gently pull apart the shell and lift the lobster meat, leaving it attached at the tail end. Place the lobster meat on top of the shell.
2. **Make the stuffing:**
   - In a small bowl, combine melted butter, minced garlic, breadcrumbs, Parmesan cheese, chopped parsley, salt, and pepper. Mix until well combined.
3. **Stuff the lobster tails:**
   - Spoon the breadcrumb mixture evenly over the top of each lobster tail, pressing gently to adhere.
4. **Bake the lobster tails:**
   - Place the stuffed lobster tails on the prepared baking sheet. Bake in the preheated oven for 15-18 minutes, or until the lobster meat is opaque and cooked through, and the topping is golden brown and crispy.
5. **Serve:**
   - Remove the baked stuffed lobster tails from the oven. Serve hot, garnished with lemon wedges.

Baked stuffed lobster tails are best served immediately while they are hot and fresh from the oven. They make an impressive and delicious main course for your Christmas dinner, sure to impress your guests with its rich flavors and elegant presentation. Enjoy this decadent seafood dish as part of your holiday celebration!

Roasted Asparagus with Lemon

Ingredients:

- 1 lb (450g) fresh asparagus spears, tough ends trimmed
- 2 tablespoons olive oil
- Zest of 1 lemon
- Juice of 1/2 lemon
- Salt and freshly ground black pepper, to taste
- Grated Parmesan cheese (optional), for serving
- Lemon wedges, for serving

Instructions:

1. **Preheat the oven:**
    - Preheat your oven to 400°F (200°C).
2. **Prepare the asparagus:**
    - Place the trimmed asparagus spears on a large baking sheet in a single layer.
3. **Season the asparagus:**
    - Drizzle olive oil evenly over the asparagus spears. Toss to coat them thoroughly.
    - Sprinkle lemon zest over the asparagus. Squeeze lemon juice evenly over the spears.
    - Season with salt and freshly ground black pepper to taste.
4. **Roast the asparagus:**
    - Place the baking sheet in the preheated oven and roast the asparagus for 12-15 minutes, or until the spears are tender and lightly browned, shaking the pan halfway through for even cooking.
5. **Serve:**
    - Remove the roasted asparagus from the oven. Transfer to a serving platter.
    - Optionally, sprinkle grated Parmesan cheese over the hot asparagus for added flavor.
    - Serve immediately with lemon wedges on the side for extra zest.

Roasted asparagus with lemon is a delightful and healthy side dish that complements a variety of main courses, from roasted meats to seafood. It adds a burst of fresh flavors and vibrant color to your Christmas dinner table. Enjoy this simple yet delicious recipe with your family and friends during the holiday season!

Pistachio Crusted Rack of Lamb

Ingredients:

- 2 racks of lamb, trimmed (about 1.5 lbs each)
- Salt and freshly ground black pepper
- 2 tablespoons Dijon mustard
- 1 cup shelled pistachios, finely chopped
- 2 tablespoons breadcrumbs (panko or regular)
- 2 cloves garlic, minced
- 2 tablespoons fresh rosemary, chopped
- 2 tablespoons olive oil

Instructions:

1. **Preheat the oven:**
    - Preheat your oven to 400°F (200°C).
2. **Prepare the lamb racks:**
    - Season the racks of lamb generously with salt and pepper on all sides.
3. **Coat with Dijon mustard:**
    - Brush the lamb racks all over with Dijon mustard. Make sure to coat the meat evenly.
4. **Prepare the pistachio crust:**
    - In a bowl, combine the finely chopped pistachios, breadcrumbs, minced garlic, chopped rosemary, and olive oil. Mix well until the ingredients are evenly distributed and form a coarse paste.
5. **Coat the lamb racks with the pistachio crust:**
    - Press the pistachio mixture onto the mustard-coated surface of the lamb racks, covering them thoroughly. Pat the crust gently to adhere.
6. **Sear the lamb racks:**
    - Heat a large oven-safe skillet or frying pan over medium-high heat. Add a bit of olive oil to coat the pan. Once hot, sear the lamb racks, fat-side down first, for 2-3 minutes per side until the crust is golden brown.
7. **Roast the lamb racks:**
    - Transfer the skillet with the seared lamb racks into the preheated oven. Roast for 15-20 minutes for medium-rare (internal temperature of 135°F/57°C), or adjust cooking time according to your preferred doneness.
8. **Rest and serve:**
    - Remove the lamb racks from the oven and let them rest on a cutting board, tented with foil, for about 10 minutes. This allows the juices to redistribute.
9. **Slice and serve:**
    - Slice the pistachio-crusted rack of lamb into individual chops and arrange on a serving platter. Serve hot as a main course for your Christmas dinner.

This pistachio-crusted rack of lamb is flavorful and tender, with a crunchy, nutty crust that complements the richness of the lamb perfectly. It makes a stunning centerpiece for your holiday feast and is sure to impress your guests with its delicious taste and elegant presentation. Enjoy this festive dish with your loved ones during your Christmas celebration!

Tiramisu

Ingredients:

- 6 egg yolks
- 3/4 cup granulated sugar
- 1 cup mascarpone cheese, at room temperature
- 1 1/2 cups heavy cream
- 1 teaspoon vanilla extract
- 2 cups brewed espresso or strong coffee, cooled
- 1/2 cup coffee liqueur (such as Kahlua or Tia Maria)
- 24-30 ladyfinger cookies (savoiardi)
- Unsweetened cocoa powder, for dusting

Instructions:

1. **Prepare the mascarpone mixture:**
   - In a large bowl, whisk together the egg yolks and sugar until thick and pale in color.
2. **Add mascarpone cheese:**
   - Add the mascarpone cheese to the egg yolk mixture and beat until smooth and creamy. Set aside.
3. **Whip the heavy cream:**
   - In a separate bowl, whip the heavy cream and vanilla extract until stiff peaks form.
4. **Combine mascarpone and whipped cream:**
   - Gently fold the whipped cream into the mascarpone mixture until smooth and well combined. Be careful not to deflate the mixture.
5. **Prepare the coffee mixture:**
   - In a shallow dish, combine the cooled brewed espresso or strong coffee with the coffee liqueur.
6. **Assemble the Tiramisu:**
   - Quickly dip each ladyfinger into the coffee mixture, ensuring they are soaked but not soggy. Arrange a layer of soaked ladyfingers in the bottom of a 9x13 inch (23x33 cm) dish.
7. **Layering:**
   - Spread half of the mascarpone mixture evenly over the ladyfingers.
8. **Repeat layers:**
   - Repeat with another layer of soaked ladyfingers and remaining mascarpone mixture.
9. **Chill:**
   - Cover the Tiramisu with plastic wrap and refrigerate for at least 4 hours, preferably overnight, to allow the flavors to meld together and for the dessert to set.
10. **Dust with cocoa powder:**

- Before serving, dust the top of the Tiramisu with unsweetened cocoa powder using a fine mesh sieve.
11. **Serve:**
    - Slice and serve the Tiramisu chilled, with a dusting of cocoa powder on top.

Tiramisu is a delightful, creamy dessert with layers of flavors from coffee, mascarpone, and cocoa, making it a perfect ending to a festive Christmas dinner. Enjoy this classic Italian treat with your family and friends during your holiday celebration!

Pecan Pie

Ingredients:

- 1 9-inch (23 cm) unbaked pie crust (homemade or store-bought)
- 1 cup granulated sugar
- 1 cup light corn syrup
- 1/4 cup unsalted butter, melted
- 3 large eggs, beaten
- 1 teaspoon vanilla extract
- 1 1/2 cups pecan halves

Instructions:

1. **Preheat the oven:**
   - Preheat your oven to 350°F (175°C).
2. **Prepare the pie crust:**
   - If using a store-bought pie crust, place it in a 9-inch pie dish and crimp the edges. If using a homemade crust, roll out the dough and place it in the pie dish, then crimp the edges.
3. **Make the filling:**
   - In a medium bowl, whisk together the granulated sugar, corn syrup, melted butter, beaten eggs, and vanilla extract until well combined.
4. **Add pecans:**
   - Stir in the pecan halves until they are evenly coated with the mixture.
5. **Assemble the pie:**
   - Pour the pecan filling into the prepared pie crust, spreading it out evenly.
6. **Bake the pie:**
   - Place the pie on a baking sheet to catch any drips. Bake in the preheated oven for 50-60 minutes, or until the filling is set. The pie should jiggle slightly in the center but not be liquidy.
7. **Cool and serve:**
   - Remove the pecan pie from the oven and let it cool completely on a wire rack before serving. The filling will continue to set as it cools.
8. **Serve:**
   - Slice and serve the pecan pie at room temperature or slightly warmed, optionally with a dollop of whipped cream or a scoop of vanilla ice cream.

Pecan pie is a decadent and sweet dessert that's perfect for any holiday gathering, including Christmas dinner. Enjoy the rich flavors of buttery crust, sweet filling, and crunchy pecans in every bite!

www.ingramcontent.com/pod-product-compliance
Lightning Source LLC
LaVergne TN
LVHW081611060526
838201LV00054B/2191